Understanding Dyspraxia

also in this series

Understanding Motor Skills in Children with Dyspraxia, ADHD, Autism, and Other Learning Disabilities
A Guide to Improving Coordination
Lisa A. Kurtz
ISBN 978 1 84310 865 8

of related interest

Can't Play Won't Play
Simply Sizzling Ideas to get the Ball Rolling for Children with Dyspraxia
Sharon Drew and Elizabeth Atter
ISBN 978 1 84310 601 2

Developmental Coordination Disorder
Hints and Tips for the Activities of Daily Living
Morven F. Ball
ISBN 978 1 84310 090 4

Caged in Chaos
A Dyspraxic Guide to Breaking Free
Victoria Biggs
ISBN 978 1 84310 347 9

Understanding Dyspraxia

A Guide for Parents and Teachers

Second edition

Maureen Boon

Jessica Kingsley Publishers
London and Philadelphia

First edition published in 2001 by Jessica Kingsley Publishers
This edition published in 2010
by Jessica Kingsley Publishers
116 Pentonville Road
London N1 9JB, UK
and
400 Market Street, Suite 400
Philadelphia, PA 19106, USA

www.jkp.com

Library of Congress Cataloging in Publication Data
Boon, Maureen, 1949-
  Understanding dyspraxia : a guide for parents and teachers / Maureen Boon.
    p. cm.
  Revised ed. of the author's: Helping children with dyspraxia, 2000
  Includes bibliographical references and index.
  ISBN 978-1-84905-069-2 (alk. paper)
  1. Apraxia--Handbooks, manuals, etc. 2. Motor ability in children--Handbooks, manuals, etc.
  3. Movement disorders in children--Handbooks, manuals, etc. I. Boon, Maureen, 1949- Helping children with dyspraxia. II. Title.
  RJ496.A63B66 2010
  618.92'8552--dc22

                    2010006368

British Library Cataloguing in Publication Data
A CIP catalogue record for this book is available from the British Library

ISBN 978 1 84905 069 2

Printed and bound in the United States by
Thomson-Shore, Inc.

CONTENTS

ACKNOWLEDGEMENTS

I would like to thank the staff at Vranch House who were so helpful to me in writing this book. Vranch House is located in Exeter, Devon in the UK, and comprises a school for children with physical difficulties and a therapy centre for young people with a range of movement difficulties. I would also like to thank the parents and young people who shared their experiences with me and allowed me to take photographs. In addition, thanks are due to all the children who attend Vranch House and work so hard with good humour and enthusiasm.

Special thanks to the following for sharing their photographs and stories for the book: Diane Zealley, Lynette Eastwood, Mrs R.J. Coulston, Sarah Whitfield, Ian Hynds and Mrs D. Staves.

Chapter 1

WHAT IS DYSPRAXIA?

If you ask different professionals what dyspraxia is, you get different answers, depending on their field of expertise. A physiotherapist would probably say that the child in question has impaired motor performance that is not linked to any known clinical cause. A speech and language therapist might say that the child has a motor difficulty that affects his or her initiating and sequencing of sounds and words. A teacher might well describe the dyspraxic child as inattentive and lacking in concentration skills. A parent might describe his or her child as clumsy and disorganized and having poor coordination. All might be descriptions of the same child.

DEFINITIONS OF DYSPRAXIA

The Dyspraxia Foundation (see Appendix 2) defines dyspraxia as 'an impairment or immaturity of the organisation of movement. Associated with this there may be problems of language, perception and thought.' It is fundamentally an immaturity in the way that the brain processes information, which results in messages not being properly or fully transmitted to the body. The term 'dyspraxia' has been recognized for some time. The word is derived from the Greek and means literally the poor performance of movements. It was defined in the *American Illustrated Medical Dictionary* in 1947 as 'partial loss of ability to perform coordinated movements' (Dorland 1947, p.465). In the same year the *New Dictionary of Psychology* gave the definition: 'impairment of well-established habits as a consequence of a stroke or of other pathologies of the central nervous system' (Harriman 1947, p.113). It is clear that at that time the meaning of 'dyspraxia' was somewhat different from our understanding today. Nowadays the term often used is the more specific 'developmental dyspraxia', implying that the condition is due to the immature development of motor abilities.

Portwood defines dyspraxia as 'motor difficulties caused by percep-tual problems, especially visual-motor and kinaesthetic-motor difficulties' (Portwood 1996, p.15). McKinlay says, 'Dyspraxia is a delay or disorder of the planning and/or execution of complex movements. It may be develop-mental – part of a child's make-up – or it can be acquired at any stage in life as the result of brain illness or injury' (McKinlay 1998, p.9). I asked my colleagues working with dyspraxic children for their definitions.

A physiotherapist's definition

> Children with dyspraxia should demonstrate no hard neurological signs (i.e. damage of the central nervous system). Their motor per-formance should be at a level lower than that expected of their general learning abilities; i.e. their motor performance is out of step with their intellectual functioning.

Another physiotherapist's definition

This physiotherapist makes a distinction between developmental coordina-tion disorder and dyspraxia:

> Developmental coordination disorder is an umbrella term for a range of movement disorders that is not due to any obvious neurological or orthopaedic condition. There may be associated difficulties with social skills, attention control, self-help skills and perceptual skills.
>
> Dyspraxia is a specific movement disorder characterized by dif-ficulty in performing an unlearned complex motor skill that may be due to difficulty with ideation, or motor planning and sequencing or the execution of the task. The disorder is often associated with poor visual or auditory and/or kinaesthetic perception.

Other disorders that she includes under developmental coordination dis-order are general global delay (i.e. learning difficulties), poor muscle tone, attention deficit hyperactivity disorder (ADHD) and general poor attention control.

An occupational therapist's definition

> Children with dyspraxia have motor coordination problems. They often present as having problems with the organization and execution of gross and fine movement. They often have associated difficulties

with perceptual and organizational skills and may have receptive and expressive language problems.

A speech and language therapist's definition

'Dyspraxia' is a term used to describe a motor problem that causes difficulty with initiation and/or sequencing of the muscle movements required to produce voice and/or speech. It is essentially a problem of not being able voluntarily to carry out movements that can easily be carried out involuntarily. A child may not be able to control and sequence breathing and voice and so only produce random vocalizations. He may not be able to move his tongue and lips into the correct positions or sequence of positions to make sounds, words or sentences, even though there is no muscle weakness to prevent this. A child can be observed to be licking his lips without realising while playing, but put on the spot and asked to lick his lips he cannot do so. Children who have the range of difficulties associated with dyspraxia often experience social-communication problems and difficulty in understanding the more abstract and subtle parts of language.

A teacher's definition

Dyspraxia is a movement disorder not caused by a known clinical condition. The children affected are within the normal range of intellectual functioning and have poor hand–eye coordination and poor gross motor coordination. It can also affect speech.

TERMS USED TO DESCRIBE DYSPRAXIA

Since the 1970s a number of different terms have been used to describe the condition which we would now term 'developmental dyspraxia', as well as other, very similar, conditions:

- Clumsy child syndrome.

- Developmental agnosia and apraxia.

- Developmental coordination disorder (DCD).

- Learning difficulties/disabilities/disorders.

- Minimal cerebral palsy.

- Minimal cerebral dysfunction.

- Minimal brain dysfunction.

- Minimal motor dysfunction.

- Motor learning difficulties.

- Neurodevelopmental dysfunction.

- Perceptual/perceptuo-motor dysfunction.

- Physical awkwardness.

- Specific learning difficulties.

- Sensori-motor dysfunction.

The number of terms used to describe dyspraxia is large and wide-ranging, and some are now used to describe quite different areas of difficulty. 'Specific learning difficulties' is a term now often taken to mean 'dyslexia' or 'dyscalculia'. Dyslexia describes specific problems with reading and recognizing written text, and dyscalculia describes difficulties with numeracy. Some terms are too vague, such as 'learning difficulties', and some are not accurate, such as 'minimal cerebral palsy'. Some are very descriptive but are not in common usage and may be considered insensitive or 'politically incorrect', for example clumsy child syndrome. The term 'developmental coordination disorder' (DCD) is the one most often used, and was first listed by the American Psychiatric Association in 1987. DCD is described as 'a marked impairment in the development of motor coordination' and it states that 'this impairment significantly interferes with academic achievement or activities of daily living'. In addition, 'the coordination difficulties are not due to a general medical condition' (American Psychiatric Association 2000, pp.56–7).

This was first endorsed by the World Health Organization in 1989 and described as 'specific developmental disorder of motor function' (World Health Organization 2007). The term is now being used interchangeably with 'developmental dyspraxia', although some use it more widely to include dyspraxia and other movement disorders.

In 1994, an international panel of health professional experts met and formed the London (Ontario) Consensus. From this meeting a statement was made to define the existence of developmental coordination disorder and describe the condition in a more detailed way. Following this, the Leeds Consensus led by Professor D.A. Sugden made a further statement in 2006 entitled *Development Coordination Disorder as a Specific Learning Difficulty*, where clinical diagnosis criteria were given (Sugden 2006). Children with DCD were said to show 'a marked impairment in the performance of motor skills' which 'has a significant, negative impact on activities of daily living – such as dressing, feeding, riding a bicycle – and/or on academic achievement such as through poor handwriting skills' (Sugden 2006, pp.3, 4). It was also stated that 'DCD is a unique and separate neurodevelopmental disorder' although it can be present alongside other developmental disorders (Sugden 2006, p.5). The Leeds Consensus recommended that practitioners assess children using 'an individually administered and culturally appropriate, norm refer-enced test of general motor competence' and that performance should be at or below the fifth percentile (i.e. in the bottom 20%). It also recommended that children with an IQ of below 70 should not be given a diagnosis of DCD. An IQ of below 70 indicates significant learning difficulties – the average for children overall being 100.

The term DCD is the preferred term for children with dyspraxia used by most medical clinicians.

DIFFERENT TYPES OR ASPECTS OF DYSPRAXIA

A number of types or aspects of dyspraxia have been described.

Verbal dyspraxia

With verbal dyspraxia the child has difficulty in actually carrying out the movements needed to produce clear speech. Not all children with dyspraxia have difficulties with speech and language. Sometimes the child may have difficulty in actually producing the sounds or may be able to produce them at some times but not at others. The child may find copying speech more difficult than when using speech spontaneously. Sometimes the child has difficulty in producing the right word at the right time and putting the words in the right order.

Sensory integrative dysfunction

Sensory Integrative Therapy was pioneered by Dr A. Jean Ayres, an American occupational therapist (Ayres 1972). Children with sensory integrative dysfunction have difficulties in sensory integration, which means that they find it difficult to organize the information received from the sensory apparatus about the interaction of their body with the environment.

That is to say, the difficulty is in making sense of the information received from the senses of hearing, sight, smell, touch and taste and through the proprioception system and the vestibular apparatus. Proprioceptors are nerve endings, or receptors, through which we are aware of our muscles and joints and whether they are bending or stretching. The vestibular apparatus, which is in the inner ear, gives information about movement and our position in space. It is the system through which we are aware of the position of our head in relation to gravity. Through kinaesthetic sensations we become aware of the relationship between body parts, joint positions and movements.

Poor sensory integration may mean that some dyspraxic children are oversensitive to noise or to different textures. Some may not be able to perform certain movements unless they can observe the body part moving. For example, if children are asked to stretch out an arm in front of them and then asked to place a finger on their nose, they may be able to do this with their eyes open when they can observe the moving hand, but not if they close their eyes.

Ideational dyspraxia and ideomotor dyspraxia

Ripley, Daines and Barrett (1997) describe two areas of difficulty as ideational and ideomotor dyspraxia. With ideational dyspraxia, the child has difficulties in planning sequential coordinated movements (Ripley *et al.* 1997, p.5). With ideomotor dyspraxia, the child knows what to do but has difficulties in carrying out a plan of action.

THE INCIDENCE OF DYSPRAXIA

The first time I heard the word 'clumsy' used to describe a group of children was when I was working as a substitute teacher in a school for children with physical disabilities in 1978. I was taking lessons for the deputy head, who was on a week's course on 'Teaching the Clumsies'. In 1983 I returned to work at the same school as head of lower school, and at that time this group of children with less severe physical difficulties had become smaller through integration into mainstream schools, and they were rarely referred to as 'clumsy'.

Since 1983 I have worked with children with motor disorders in both special and mainstream schools, and it was only when I moved to my current school, Vranch House, in Devon in 1992 that I heard the term 'dyspraxia' being used commonly and on an everyday basis. Since 1999 'dyspraxia' has been used more frequently in books and journals and has replaced the awkward, somewhat negative but descriptive word, 'clumsy'. As mentioned above the term DCD or developmental coordination disorder is the one most favoured by medical clinicians and a term many parents may hear introduced during therapeutic interventions.

In 1988–1989 I carried out a study on the integration of children with special needs in mainstream schools (Boon 1993), which involved studying registers of all children who had a statement of special educational needs and were included in mainstream schools in Lancashire, northern England, and classifying them by special educational need. The statement of special educational needs is a way of extra support or funding being allocated to a child with identified additional needs. The registers made no mention of dyspraxia. One child was described as 'disorganized'. All the others fell under the headings of specific, moderate or severe learning difficulties; sensory, language or physical difficulties; or emotional/behavioural difficulties. Nowadays I would expect a similar study to describe a fair number of children as 'dyspraxic'.

At Vranch House the therapy department sees every year on average 250 new children from mainstream schools who would be described as having DCD. These children are all referred for gross and fine motor skill difficulties although only about 20 per cent would fit the definition of a diagnosis of DCD.

In her Durham study Portwood (1996) suggests an incidence of 6 per cent out of the whole population. In their Leeds study Roussounis, Gaussen and Stratton (1987) found that the incidence of 'clumsy children' was 8.5 per cent from a cohort of 200 children at primary school entry age. In a study of schoolchildren in East Kent, Dussart (1994) found the incidence to be between 3.7 and 6.5 per cent, depending on whether the results were based on the TOMI, or Test of Motor Impairment (Stott, Moyes and Henderson 1984) or on a checklist developed by Dussart for the study. Different estimates are, however, likely to be dependent on the screening measures used. The more recent version of the TOMI is the Movement Assessment Battery for Children – Second Edition (Movement ABC-2) (Henderson and Sugden 2007). It is commonly used in the UK and the US, and children who score on or below the fifth percentile are normally considered to be those needing intervention. As the test is standardized, this necessarily means that the incidence will be around 5 per cent.

Sugden (2008) gave the incidence as 6 per cent but said that this figure depended on the test used, the cut-off point of the test and the reason the assessor is looking for incidence which could be needs or resource led (i.e. dependent on either the needs of the child or on the resources available).

The ratio of boys to girls has always shown a higher percentage of boys than girls. Gordon and McKinlay (1980) found that of 'clumsy' children referred to the neurology clinics of the children's hospitals in Manchester the ratio of boys to girls was four to one. Portwood (1996) found the ratio to be the same. Sugden (2008) suggested a ratio of two to one. This level of incidence means that in the average primary school class of 28 pupils there is likely to be at least one pupil with dyspraxia who is probably a boy.

DIFFICULTIES EXPERIENCED BY CHILDREN WITH DYSPRAXIA

Dyspraxic children may experience difficulties in some or all of the following areas.

Gross motor skills

Dyspraxic children may move awkwardly and have poor balance and co-ordination. They may bump into things and bruise themselves without being aware of this. They may have difficulties in physical education (PE) generally. Activities such as climbing up ropes and ladders, balancing on a beam or bench, or walking along a line can cause problems. Any kind of locomotion activity in gymnastics and dance can be a challenge when pupils are often asked to vary speed, pattern of movement and levels. Working cooperatively with a partner calls for even more control. They are likely to have poor ball skills, when using either hands or feet for skills such as catching and throwing and kicking a ball. All these difficulties make team games particularly difficult and they may not get selected for teams.

Fine motor skills

Dyspraxic children may find holding pencils and pens difficult, and their writing and drawing may be poorly formed. Scissors are another source of difficulty. Drawing lines with rulers is quite a complex skill which may cause problems. Painting pictures with paints and paint brushes can become a mess both on paper and on the child. Construction toys may be difficult to handle. Children may find cutlery and other mealtime utensils hard to manage and make a mess. Dressing skills such as fastening zips, buttons and laces may be very difficult or impossible. They may use strategies to put clothes on that make them look untidy and out of shape, such as putting shoes on without undoing them and thus treading down the backs of the shoes, or always pulling clothes on or off without fastening or unfastening them so that they lose buttons and the clothes look stretched and out of shape. They may find it difficult to thread beads, build with small bricks or use other toys that need reasonably fine motor skills. This may make play frustrating and cause them to become angry that they cannot do things which they see other children doing easily.

Speech and language

Dyspraxic children may have unclear speech, which may be immature and difficult to understand, causing other children to ignore them or tease them. They may find it difficult to put their ideas into words and this can cause them frustration. They sometimes seem to miss or not understand what is said to them.

Social skills

All the above have an effect on their social skills. Dyspraxic children may find it difficult to make friends and to be part of a group. Their difficulty with motor skills will mean that they are not often chosen to play games where these skills are necessary. Their speech and language difficulties may result in other children teasing or ignoring them. If they do not understand what is said to them, they may not get the gist of what everyone is talking about and miss out on an activity which they would have enjoyed.

Attention and concentration

Dyspraxic children find it difficult to concentrate for very long. They may be easily distracted by noises, things happening outside the classroom window or other activities going on around them. They may find it difficult to sit still. Sitting on a carpet for circle time or a story may be particularly difficult. They may ask to go to the toilet frequently as they need to stretch their legs and move.

Learning

Dyspraxic children may have difficulties with reading, spelling and maths, which may be linked to poor visual-perceptual skills. In reading they may find it difficult to match and recognize letters and words. They may find it very difficult to set out work in maths and when writing due to their poor fine motor skills and difficulties with visual-spatial relationships. Following complicated instructions given by the teacher can be perplexing and lead to the child being labelled as inattentive or careless.

Visual-motor skills

Dyspraxic children may find it difficult to copy pictures, patterns, writing or movements. They may have poor spatial awareness. These skills are essential in the development of reading, numeracy and handwriting. Readiness for handwriting is essential. If children are taught handwriting at too early a stage, they become frustrated and will develop poor writing skills which become ingrained and difficult to correct.

Chapter 2

WHAT CAUSES DYSPRAXIA?

It is not clearly known what causes dyspraxia. It appears to be a developmental delay specifically in areas affecting motor function, which may involve gross motor, fine motor or articulatory skills. Some dyspraxic children also have other learning difficulties, while some are of average or above-average intelligence. Some practitioners would argue that a child who has a moderate general learning difficulty is effectively delayed globally and therefore is not dyspraxic. Kate Ripley says that 'Developmental Dyspraxia is found in children who have no significant difficulties when assessed using standard neurological examinations but who show signs of an impaired performance of skilled movements' (Ripley 2001, p.1). However, treatment has also proved effective with children who have a range of learning difficulties but demonstrate typical 'dyspraxic' features in their motor development. The Leeds Consensus (Sugden 2006) judged that DCD was idiopathic (i.e. had no known cause).

Wedell points out that 'the development of sensory and motor organisation starts before language development' (Wedell 1973, p.46). It is clear that any delays in sensory and motor organization will affect all areas of subsequent learning. In some instances it is difficult to say how much a child's motor disorder has contributed to his or her other learning difficulties.

REASONS GIVEN FOR DYSPRAXIA

The Dyspraxia Foundation says:

> For the majority of those with the condition, there is no known cause. Current research suggests that it is due to an immaturity of neurone development in the brain rather than to brain damage. People with dyspraxia have no clinical neurological abnormality to explain their condition.

Madeleine Portwood agrees with this: 'Dyspraxia results when parts of the brain have failed to mature properly…[it] is the result of neurological immaturity in the cortex of the brain' (Portwood 1999, pp.5, 11). When describing 'clumsiness' Barnett *et al.* (1989) say: 'Medical evidence suggests that defects in the receiving and passing on of messages to and from the brain result in lack of co-ordination of eyesight and bodily movement, and sometimes cause speech disorders' (Barnett *et al.* 1989, p.50).

With regard to developmental verbal dyspraxia, Rosenthal and McCabe (1999) comment:

> At one time people thought dyspraxia was caused by brain damage, but this has not been shown to be the case. The fact that it often occurs in several family members makes it unlikely for brain damage to be the usual cause. A very small number of children have dyspraxia as a result of other problems including galactosaemia [an adverse reaction to milk which can give rise to symptoms such as cataracts, visual impairment, gastro-intestinal disorders and jaundice], global developmental delay etc. but most are of an undetermined cause. (Rosenthal and McCabe 1999, p.3)

WHAT DOES ALL THIS MEAN?

As there are usually no identifiable neurological signs to indicate dyspraxia, so the reasons given for the difficulties are all somewhat speculative. As mentioned in Chapter 1, it is thought that some dyspraxic children have difficulties with sensory integration. Children receive a variety of information through the senses – for example, from what they see, hear, feel by touch or feel within their body in relation to gravity. They then have to integrate all these sensations in order to plan and carry out an action.

Young children learn many motor skills by cause and effect. For example, if they touch a toy hanging in their cot or pram something may happen. The toy may move or make a noise. This is initially an accidental response which becomes learned and subsequently relies upon the babies' ability to look and reach out with their hand and coordinate the acts of looking and reaching.

If babies have difficulty in integrating the information received from their senses, their ability to learn by cause and effect may be delayed. If learning is affected by a movement delay, as described in Chapter 1, pupils are likely to be perceived as having learning difficulties. If their motor abilities improve, this will clearly affect all areas of learning. The key therefore is to provide the right movement programme to help these pupils to give them the skills to become movement literate.

PHYSICAL LITERACY

The Programme for International Student Assessment (PISA 2003) defines 'reading literacy' as 'the ability to understand, use and reflect on written texts in order to achieve one's goals, to develop one's knowledge and potential, and to participate effectively in society' (p.19). 'Mathematical literacy' is defined as 'the capacity to identify, understand and engage in mathematics as well as to make well-founded judgements about the role that mathematics plays in an individual's current and future life as a constructive, concerned and reflective citizen' (p.20). 'Scientific literacy' is defined as 'the capacity to use scientific knowledge, to identify questions and to draw evidence-based conclusions in order to understand and help make decisions about the natural world and human interactions with it' (p.21).

In a similar way I would define 'movement literacy' as the ability to engage in movement experiences effectively, to use those experiences to make sense of the world around and to enable the individual to fully participate in other associated learning experiences.

The term 'physical literacy' is relatively new but one which is becoming a frequently heard expression within education across the world. Dr Margaret Whitehead has set up the website Physical Literacy (www.physical-literacy.org.uk) 'to enable all those interested in the concept of Physical Literacy to share thoughts and references'. Whitehead describes physical literacy as 'the motivation, confidence, physical competence, knowledge and understanding to maintain physical activity throughout life'. Whitehead describes a person who is physically literate:

> The person moves with poise, economy and confidence in a wide variety of physically challenging situations. In addition the individual is perceptive in 'reading' all aspects of the physical environment, anticipating movement needs or possibilities and responding appropriately to these, with intelligence and imagination. ...Physical Literacy requires a holistic engagement that encompasses physical capacities embedded in perception, experience, memory, anticipation and decision making. (Whitehead 2001)

Whitehead also acknowledges the importance of physical literacy being relative to a person's individual abilities.

The Canadian Sport Centre describes physical literacy as 'the development of fundamental movement skills...and fundamental sport skills... that permit a child to move confidently and with control, in a wide range of physical activity, rhythmic (dance) and sport situations' (Higgs *et al.* 2008, p.5).

Sport Northern Ireland defines physical literacy as 'the ability to use body management, locomotor and object control skills in a competent manner, with the capacity to apply them with confidence in settings which may lead to sustained involvement in sport and physical recreation' (Delaney *et al.* 2008, p.2).

There is a general movement within education to improve children's fitness and well-being. Some of the definitions above are specifically related to improving abilities within sport. This is why I personally prefer the term 'movement literacy', which is related to children's ability to develop skills to support them in their everyday lives.

HEALTHY SCHOOLS AND HEALTHY CHILDREN

In 1999 the UK government introduced the Healthy Schools Programme. This was a joint initiative between the Department for Children, Schools and Families (DCSF) and Department of Health (DH). The aim was to promote a whole school and whole child approach to health. Schools were encouraged to achieve 'Healthy School Status' by fulfilling a number of criteria across four themes:

- Personal, social, health and economic (PSHE) education, including sex and relationship education (SRE) and drugs education.

- Healthy eating.

- Physical activity.

- Emotional health and well-being, including bullying.

Under 'Physical activity' schools were encouraged to give pupils a range of physical activities within school and understand the importance of physical activity to leading a healthy life. A very similar initiative in the US is the Healthier US School Challenge. Schools can earn four levels of award (Bronze, Silver, Gold or Distinction) by enrolling as a Team Nutrition School, offering healthy lunches, providing nutrition education and ensuring students have opportunities for physical education and activity. See Appendix 1 for details.

These initiatives have had a major effect on schools and their families by encouraging children to take more exercise and eat healthier diets. There have been a number of local initiatives in south-west England, including:

- Leap into Life in Devon.

- DASH in Somerset.

- Family Fun Fit in Cornwall.

Leap into Life (Devon Curriculum Services, see Appendix 1 for details) is a school-based four-year dynamic movement programme for the Foundation Stage and Key Stage 1 (pre-school, kindergarten and first grade in the US) which is aimed to improve physical literacy for pupils aged four to seven years old. DASH stands for 'Do Activity Stay Healthy' and was set up as an early morning exercise class. Its aim is for the school and family to work together through physical activity and health education. The programme was developed by the Somerset Activity and Sports Partnership (SASP) and Somerset Coast Primary Care Trust. Family Fun Fit is a school-based family activity scheme aimed to improve fitness levels in parents and their children. See Appendix 2 for further details of these programmes.

More recently in 2009 the National Institute for Health and Clinical Excellence (NICE) has published a document entitled *Promoting Physical Activity, Active Play and Sport for Pre-school and School-age Children and Young People in Family, Pre-school, School and Community Settings* (NICE 2009). This document was produced at the request of the Department of Health and recommends a long-term UK campaign 'to promote physical activity among children and young people' (NICE 2009, p.10). NICE stresses that physical activity should be 'healthy, fun and enjoyable and help to promote independence and to develop movement skills'.

Alongside the Healthy Schools initiative is the *Every Child Matters* agenda (DfES 2004) which now has an entire website devoted to it (see Appendix 1 for details). The *Every Child Matters* outcomes were divided into five areas:

- Be healthy.

- Stay safe.

- Enjoy and achieve.

- Make a positive contribution.

- Achieve economic well-being.

This initiative has been very influential in schools in the UK and two aspects of 'Be healthy' are physical health and healthy lifestyles. These have also caught the interest of the press and even TV chefs and athletes, who have been actively involved in attempting to improve children's nutrition and physical fitness.

In her book *Toxic Childhood*, Sue Palmer (2006, p.3) highlights the importance of a healthy lifestyle including more physical exercise, outdoor activity and play and links this to what she describes as 'The "special needs" explosion' including children with dyspraxia.

Chapter 3

WHAT ARE CHILDREN
WITH DYSPRAXIA LIKE?

Boys are four times more likely to be affected by dyspraxia than girls. As the dyspraxic child is usually a boy, from now on we will refer to the child with dyspraxia as 'he'. In the first two sections of this chapter we will assume that the child being described is now about six or seven years old, which is often the age at which he begins to experience real difficulties in school.

AT HOME

As a baby he was slow at sitting, crawling and walking. Some dyspraxic children do not crawl. One twin boy I met was very efficient at moving everywhere on his bottom and was perfectly happy with this method of locomotion at home. However, when he was taken out with his twin sister, who could walk, he got very frustrated that she was allowed to get out and walk but he had to stay in the buggy.

The dyspraxic child may be slow at talking and may get frustrated that he cannot make his feelings and wishes known.

As a schoolchild he takes ages to get dressed in the mornings. He cannot tie his laces and will not even consider trying. Even though he now has Velcro fastenings on his shoes, he is reluctant to use them and tends to force his feet into the already fastened shoes that he shrugged off the night before. He sometimes gets them on the wrong feet and does not realize. He forgets to bring his reading book home from school. He cannot remember his homework. He is not sure on which day he has to take his PE kit. He always looks a mess when he comes home from school, with his clothes generally untidy, his shirt hanging out and his jumper sometimes inside out or back to front. He often has dirty hands and face. He tends to get into fights and disputes with other children over seemingly trivial issues. It is never his fault and he says people are 'not fair' to him. He may have difficulties eating without making a mess. Cutlery can be a problem and his chewing may be 'messy'.

As he gets older and more familiar with the school timetable, he may complain of headaches or stomach aches on problem days – for example, PE day. He sometimes complains that music or household appliances are noisy. He still startles at loud noises. He may find that some textures of clothing irritate his skin.

IN PRIMARY OR ELEMENTARY SCHOOL
Handwriting and fine motor activities
In school the teacher is likely to notice that the dyspraxic child has poor handwriting and his work is generally untidy. He hardly ever has a pen or pencil available, and if he does his pencil needs sharpening. He often breaks it because he presses so hard when he is writing. His drawing is also messy, and not very recognizable. He may have great problems with the use of scissors, even 'special' ones. He never seems to be able to complete written work in time.

Physical education
He finds PE difficult. He finds it hard to throw and catch any sort of ball. He cannot skip, and finds kicking a ball difficult. He sometimes makes odd compensatory movements with his hands and arms – for example, when running. 'Left' and 'right' often seem to be a problem when these terms are used. He also confuses positional words such as 'in front', 'behind' and 'beside'. He is always the last one to get picked when the children are choosing partners or teams. He often scorns an activity as 'easy', although when he tries he finds it very difficult – for example, kicking a football accurately into a goal area.

He finds it hard to follow rules. Sometimes this is due to a total misunderstanding, as he has not listened carefully or understood the explanation given by the teacher. Sometimes he breaks the rules out of sheer frustration; for example, he never gets near the ball in a game of football and so he picks it up and takes it away.

He takes absolutely ages to get changed, both before and after PE. When the class has been swimming he may find it easier just to put his trousers on over his swimming trunks, or to take his trunks off and then 'forget' to put on his pants and even his socks.

Other classroom activities

He tends to be clumsy and to knock things over such as paint pots, and he scatters small maths equipment everywhere. He often bumps into other children when moving around the classroom or when running around the playground. The other children sometimes get annoyed about this. He always seems to be fidgeting and is unable to sit still; the worst time is when the class have to sit on the carpet. He gets uncomfortable and wriggles around; he cannot concentrate on what the teacher is saying and knocks into the other children, who get annoyed with him.

He cannot beat a rhythm in music, handles musical instruments awkwardly, and tends to play louder than the other children. He often forgets to bring his reading book and PE kit to school and frequently loses them.

He sometimes starts laughing and messing around during lessons when the children are supposed to be concentrating on written work. He usually finds someone willing to join him in this disruptive activity. At other times he does not seem to have many friends. When the teacher asks, 'Who did that?' regarding a misdemeanour, the children usually say, 'He did it' automatically.

He may have speech difficulties, which makes it difficult for his teacher and his classmates to understand him. He may get very frustrated when he is not understood or when his classmates mimic him or laugh at him. Sometimes he just cannot think of the word he wants to say and this may make him cross when other children answer for him. His difficulties in discriminating and sequencing phonic sounds may also affect his reading. Similarly, he finds it even more difficult putting his ideas into writing than putting his thoughts into words. He may have trouble with sequencing and time-related activities such as learning the days of the week, the months and the seasons and the concepts of before and after.

His general awkwardness with equipment and problems with positional words often mean that some numerical concepts pose difficulties for him. Completing maths worksheets can be a problem because he finds it hard to form numerals and to carry out simple mapping activities which involve him drawing lines from one object to another. Using a ruler is extremely difficult as he has to hold it still with one hand while drawing a straight line against it with the other, consequently most of his lines are crooked and wildly inaccurate.

His frustration at not being able to do things he wants to do, combined with low self-esteem, makes him irritable and prone to outbursts of temper. He may also be excitable and seem unable to sit still. He will often find strategies for getting out of tasks that he finds difficult, such as writing. He may ask to go to the toilet or lose his equipment and ask to go and find it.

MOVING TO SECONDARY, MIDDLE OR JUNIOR HIGH SCHOOL

Getting around

The child now finds himself in a much larger and more confusing environment. Instead of one teacher who knows him well, he now has a number of teachers, some of whom he may see only once a week. Sometimes he is moving around the school with his class and can follow them, but at other times they may be split into sets and join up with other children. Sometimes the boys may go one way while the girls go another, as for example for sport or PE. He initially finds the geography of the school confusing. The timetable is puzzling and he finds it hard to follow. Another major problem is organizing his large, heavy school bag and carrying it around school. If he is lucky the school may have a locker system where he can store his bag but that doesn't help when he needs to reorganize his materials at break and lunchtime – putting away some books and equipment and finding items for the next lesson.

At lunchtime he has to queue for his meal, hold a tray and select and pay for his food while possibly still carrying his bag. There may be rules which he finds difficult to follow, such as keeping to the left or right of the corridor.

Writing

His writing was never very neat and it took him longer than most of the other children to finish things when he was at primary or elementary school, but now he finds it nearly impossible to write down the large amount of information expected of him at every lesson. He has to take notes when the teacher is talking, he has to copy information down from the board, and frequently at the end of the lesson the teacher quickly tells them to write down their homework either from dictation or from the board. He finds that the others have gone before he has finished, and he either gets into trouble for taking so long or is late for his next lesson – providing he finds where he is meant to be going, that is. When he gets home and tries to read what he wrote under pressure of time, he finds it is illegible even to him and he cannot work out what homework he is meant to do.

PE and games

There seems to be more of an emphasis on team games at school, and getting 'picked' is even more difficult especially as he still has problems catching, throwing, kicking and aiming. It sometimes seems to him a good idea to forget his PE kit and sit and watch. When he does have his kit, he still finds he takes much longer than anyone else to get changed.

Practical lessons

New problems have emerged. He is expected to use science and technology equipment, and some of the things are quite hazardous. He still tends to knock things over, and this can be rather dangerous when he is cooking or using a Bunsen burner or woodworking or metalworking tools. He is usually paired by the teacher with someone who can do the task, and so tends to watch and give advice.

PAUL: A CASE STUDY

Paul is nearly eight years old and attends his local primary school in rural Devon.[1] He is the second of two children – his brother is two years older than him. The first concern his parents had was when they realized that his speech was delayed at about three and a half years old. He was speaking a few words but not very clearly, and he was not using sentences. His mother found this odd because he was developing well in other areas. Paul was a very happy child. He was like a whirlwind, charging around, banging and crashing into things and falling over. His family put this down to him being a big, boisterous boy. He clearly loved life, was obviously a bright child and his social skills were good. He interacted well from an early age with smiling and pointing, and had good eye contact. He had, however, shown an unusual lack of a sense of danger, and at 11 months had crawled up to the edge of a drop in a friend's garden and would have lowered himself off if he had not been stopped by his mother. It was clear that he would not have been able to manage the drop safely, but he himself was not aware of this.[2]

As a baby he had never slept well and was always hard to settle; his parents did not have an unbroken night until he was three and a half years old. During the day he always napped well; he would tear around, tire himself out and then fall asleep. He also had some feeding problems. As a baby he

---

1   All the children's names have been replaced by pseudonyms in the interest of confidentiality.

2   Depth perception is normally present in babies as soon as they start to move independently (Dixon 1972; Gibson and Walk 1960).

would drink too much milk and vomit back a lot. When he started eating solid food, he still had a big appetite but would often choke on his food.

As a young child he did not like loud noises and did not like getting water on his clothes.

Paul had shown very little interest in books. He would sit in bed with his mother with a book and turn the pages as fast as he could, then crawl across the floor and get another book. Then he would get back into bed and do the same thing again. He had never picked up on nursery rhymes or joined in saying the last words of familiar repetitive stories.

His favourite game was hide-and-seek. But he would always hide in full view, on the wrong side of the tree that was supposed to be hiding him, with his hands over his face. He would then be really excited when someone found him. He could never get the counting to ten at the beginning of the game right, either.

He had crawled at the usual time, and since he was obviously a bright child his family did not really worry until a check-up when he was three and a half years old and it became clear that his speech was delayed. He was also still in nappies (diapers) at this stage. He then had some speech and language therapy, but the speech and language therapist was quite reassuring and not over-anxious about his level of development. He went to playgroup before starting school, and loved it. His mother had noticed that if they started to sit at a table to do anything, he was quickly off and playing with something else.

He then started school full time, and within two weeks he was having temper tantrums and saying everything was too hard and that he could not do it. When the speech and language therapist went into school to explain about Paul's speech delay, she saw that he had other difficulties as well. Another speech and language therapist at the same centre assessed him and said that she thought he was dyspraxic.

Paul started school in January, and during his first term he refused to go. As soon as he was being dressed in his uniform, he was taking it off again. His mother had to carry him to school to get him there. As the school is small and both the reception and Year 1 children (aged four to five) are in the same class, it was quite a structured learning environment. The children spent a lot of time sitting at their desks, which Paul hated. He found he could not do the things he was being asked to do, like getting changed for PE.

The school asked the educational psychologist to visit, and a report was received by the end of Paul's second term. His parents had also requested that he be assessed at Vranch House, and he had this assessment shortly after the end of his second term. The statementing procedure took nearly a year, and Paul had extra classroom support during his second summer term when he was in Year 1. He had an hour a day initially but this has now been increased to about two and a half hours. Please see Chapter 5 for further information about the statementing procedure.

Once the school understood about Paul's difficulties and had advice and support, the situation changed. His teacher's approach was much more flexible. She did not expect him to concentrate as long, she made allowances for him, and she praised him for good work.

When Paul was a toddler his mother had taken him to the local gym club, which he really enjoyed. There was a lot of free play and each child would have a very short individual session with the gym coach. When he was school age his mother took him back for two sessions but after that he refused to go any more. The sessions were now much more structured and he realized that he was unable to do the things the other children could do.

Paul enjoyed attending movement groups at Vranch House. It was the highlight of his week. He has learned to swim and is now very confident in the pool. He has also improved skills such as jumping, kicking a ball, throwing and catching, and his fine motor control has improved.

He took the Key Stage 1 SATs (standard assessment tests) when he was seven and was assessed in all areas as working towards level 1[3], which is well below average. Now in school less than a year later, his maths is within the normal range although probably at the lower end of his age group. His reading has improved a lot in the last six months and he is learning words well and reading books with more text. His handwriting is still something that he finds difficult. Sometimes it is quite neat but at other times it is anything but. It is very hard for Paul to produce neat work every time.

In maths he sometimes mixes up the addition and multiplication signs. He is getting quite good at number patterns and maths games and the family plays games at home which involve maths skills. They also play board games, dominoes and cards.

In the afternoons Paul's age group now go and visit the junior (Key Stage 2)[4] class to do activities such as art and science. His brother is in this older class. His mother says that Paul seems very capable now to people

---

3   In the UK all children are assessed at the end of Year 2 when they are six or seven years old. These are called standard assessment tests as all schools have to carry them out. The children are tested in English and mathematics, and can score three levels. The average level is 2b (level 2 is split into three sub-levels – 2a, 2b and 2c). Children working below the level of the SATs are assessed by teacher assessment.

4   Pupils move to Key Stage 2 when they are seven years old (similar to second grade in the US).

who are not familiar with his difficulties, and he is sometimes asked to do things that are too hard for him. For instance, he was asked to do three activities as part of a planning exercise in the junior class. He had to draw a margin, put a title at the top of the page and do a piece of writing. He was quite upset that he could not do it.

The school recently had a workshop on dyspraxia for staff, organized by the local authority (LA). The speech and language therapist still comes in weekly to see Paul and sets work for the classroom assistant to do with him.

One incident related by his mother shows Paul's determination to do things he finds difficult and demonstrates his growing self-confidence:

> They had a poetry day and the children had to take a poem in to class. In the afternoon when the parents were invited in, some of the children read their poems and Paul wasn't chosen. We had chosen a little football poem – four lines, which he'd been practising at home. When I went in he called me and said he hadn't been chosen to read his poem. At the end there was some time left and they asked who would like to read their poem. Paul had his hand up and they said he could read his.
>
> He was clattering around looking for this poem and his brother was looking too. There were my children – everyone else is sitting there, and they were clattering about trying to find his poem and David [his brother] was very concerned. Paul did eventually read his poem. He got up there and he read it – very badly. He had to be helped out, he obviously couldn't remember it, and he couldn't read it properly. He said to me afterwards, 'They didn't pick me but I got to read it.' He was proud of himself. He's full of confidence. It's odd really, but he'll work quite hard to get into a situation where he probably knows he's going to struggle – but he really wanted to do that. He got there.

Chapter 4

HOW ARE CHILDREN WITH DYSPRAXIA IDENTIFIED?

In most cases it is the parents who first wonder what is wrong, especially if the dyspraxic child is not their first. Things seem different and their child does not seem to progress at the rate they expect.

It may be when a health professional checks developmental milestones that delays are noticed. The child may be behind on gross and fine motor targets, which are the first to be demonstrable. Later, the language milestones may be delayed. The child may walk without first crawling (i.e. getting around by bottom shuffling) or may have feeding and/or sleeping problems. He may also be 'difficult' and not easy to settle, or rather hyperactive.

If the child's difficulties are recognized at the pre-school stage either by the parents or a health professional, the parents will usually meet their family doctor to discuss their concerns. Occasionally the nursery or playgroup may spot that the child is experiencing difficulties and mention this to the parents.

Following identification of a developmental disorder, the child may be referred to a paediatrician who may then refer him and his parents for specialist advice or placement at the local child development centre or children's centre. Pre-school advisory teachers may provide advice and sometimes Portage workers may provide support in the home for parents. Portage is a scheme that originated in Portage, Wisconsin, and is now widely used all over the world, including in the UK (see Appendix 2 for further information). A trained Portage worker suggests activities that a child with special needs can carry out with the help of his parents in his own home. Portage is only usually available for children who are experiencing a developmental delay of at least a year.

If the difficulties have not been picked up by the parent or a health professional, a teacher may notice problems when the child starts school. This may not come as a surprise to the parents, who may well have noticed differences well before their child started school. The school may find that the child falls over and bumps into things, is disorganized, is hopeless at getting changed, will not sit still and finds writing very difficult. Initially he may fit in, but find it very difficult when he moves from the more relaxed atmosphere of the nursery or reception class to join the Year 1 class (kindergarten to elementary school in the US). In Year 1 he is expected to pay attention, recognize routines and concentrate in group situations during the literacy and numeracy sessions. The child may be assumed by the school to have behavioural rather than movement difficulties.

Having discovered that there is a problem, the school will follow the guidelines set out in the *Special Educational Needs Code of Practice* (DfES 2001a) involving parental consultation. (The *Code of Practice* will be described in more detail in Chapter 5.) It was produced following the Education Act 1993 to give practical guidance to local education authorities and schools on assessing and helping children with special educational needs. After the school's initial assessment, advice may be requested from the educational psychologist, the social services department and the school medical officer, and via the school medical officer from health-related specialists such as a paediatrician, physiotherapist, occupational therapist or speech and language therapist. Advisory teachers may also be involved – for example, those with expertise in information and communication technology (ICT) or related special educational needs.

If the school has not taken action under the *Code of Practice*, parents who have concerns when the child is of school age can talk to his teacher, the special educational needs coordinator (SENCO, or special education teacher/educator in the US) or the headteacher. Parents can also make a formal request to the local authority to ask them to carry out a statutory assessment.

There may be a screening procedure at school entry which aims to identify children with delays in various areas of development. Dussart (1994) describes a screening procedure developed in East Kent, south-east England, to identify children with developmental coordination disorder (DCD) using a checklist completed by teachers which was followed up by using the Test of Motor Impairment (Stott *et al.* 1984). Portwood (1996) also developed a screening procedure in County Durham, north-east England, to identify children with dyspraxia. She asked teachers to screen the children using a number of criteria, and followed this up with a more detailed screening using the Wechsler Pre-school and Primary Scale of Intelligence and the Wechsler Intelligence Scale for Children (Wechsler 1990, 1992) and the

Movement Assessment Battery for Children (Henderson and Sugden 1992). An intervention programme was then carried out.

The aim of a baseline assessment is twofold: to assess each individual child's abilities and from this to plan effective programmes of work, and also to provide a baseline to measure progress as the child moves through the school.

As from September 1998 Baseline Assessment has been carried out in the UK with schoolchildren in their first year in a reception class. From 2003 this was standardized as the Foundation Stage Profile (DfES 2003). From 2009 this has become an 'e-profile' which teachers complete online. The Foundation Stage Profile is used to assess pupil progress across six areas of learning:

- Personal, social and emotional development.

- Communication, language and literacy.

- Problem solving, reasoning and numeracy.

- Knowledge and understanding of the world.

- Physical development.

- Creative development.

Teachers make judgements based on observations of consistent and independent behaviour, mainly from observing children's self-initiated activities such as play activities.

The main aim of the Early Years Foundation Stage (EYFS) Profile is to provide the child's next teacher and parents with reliable and accurate information about the level of development a child has reached at the end of the reception or foundation year and help the new teacher to plan appropriately for the child's learning.

The *Statutory Framework for the Early Years Foundation Stage* (DfES 2007) allows for children with special educational needs who are working below the level of the scales to be assessed in a different way according to the child's individual needs. The Framework says: 'The EYFS Profile is a way of summing up each child's development and learning achievements at the end of the EYFS' (DfES 2007, p.16). It is based on ongoing observation and assessment by practitioners. Parents must be provided with a written summary of the child's progress and may receive a copy of the EYFS profile on request. Many schools provide parents with a copy of the profile as a matter of course. A lot of schools have developed the profile into a very special record of a child's achievements by including photographs and samples of work.

Chapter 5

HOW ARE CHILDREN WITH DYSPRAXIA ASSESSED?

In Chapter 4 we discussed the identification of dyspraxia. Following identification, assessments may be made by various professionals. The route will be different depending on whether the child is in school or still of pre-school age.

ASSESSMENT IN EARLY EDUCATION SETTINGS

The Early Years Foundation Stage aims to provide education which gives a secure foundation for all children. 'The overarching aim of the EYFS is to help young children achieve the five Every Child Matters outcomes of staying safe, being healthy, enjoying and achieving, making a positive contribution, and achieving economic well-being' (DfES 2007, p.7). Early learning goals and educational programmes are described covering the six areas mentioned in Chapter 4:

- Personal, social and emotional development.

- Communication, language and literacy.

- Problem solving, reasoning and numeracy.

- Knowledge and understanding of the world.

- Physical development.

- Creative development.

As already mentioned, with the younger child, his paediatrician may either recommend that he visit the local child development centre (CDC) or child development services, or refer him directly to another specialist. If the child is referred to the CDC, the assessment will probably be carried out in a more informal way in a nursery setting. The CDCs normally have nursery teachers, nursery nurses, physiotherapists, speech and language therapists, occupational therapists, social workers and an educational psychologist either working at the centre or available to visit.

In addition to specialist child development centres there are now more than 3000 Sure Start Children's Centres in the UK. This initiative was launched by the UK government in 1998 and the aim is to have centres in each community to provide integrated services at a central hub to give early learning experiences, child and family health services and advice to families. This initiative is similar to the Head Start programme in the United States, Head Start in Australia and the Early Years Plan in Ontario. The Head Start programme in the US provides grants to support child development services to help economically disadvantaged children and families. Educational, health, nutritional, social and other services are made available to families. The programme prepares children to start school and involves parents in supporting their children's learning.

If the professionals working with the child feel that his needs may be significant enough to necessitate a special school placement or extra provision when he reaches school age, then they will start the statutory assessment procedure described in the *Special Educational Needs Code of Practice* (DfES 2001a), which may eventually mean the child receives a statement of special educational needs.

It is rare for a local authority to provide a statement of special educational needs for children under the age of two but parents have the right to request statutory assessment.

Within the EYFS there is now a 'graduated response' (DfES 2001a) to supporting children with special educational needs before statutory assessment commences. The first stage is 'Early Years Action' and parents must be informed at this stage. At this stage the school or pre-school provides help from its own resources. This may be in the form of extra help or working in a small group. The child should be given an individual education plan (IEP) giving details of short-term targets set for the child.

A good IEP will give details of the precise targets which are 'SMART':

- S = Specific.

- M= Measurable.

- A= Attainable.

- R= Realistic/Relevant.

- T= Time Related.

The mnemonic 'SMART' is now used commonly in education although it was originally first used in business – specifically for 'project management' (Doran 1981).

IEPs should be reviewed regularly and parents should be consulted and kept informed. If a pupil makes little or no progress or is working at a level well below that of his peers then the decision may be made to move on to 'Early Years Action Plus'. At this stage support services outside the school may be involved, for example advisory teachers, educational psychologists, therapists. Moving through the stages is usually pursued by the SENCO in consultation with the child's teacher or key worker and parents. Full statutory assessment is carried out for only a relatively small proportion of pupils who have progressed through Early Years Action and Early Years Action Plus. The child must have 'demonstrated a significant cause for concern' (DfES 2001a, p.38).

However, it is unlikely that children with dyspraxia would be recommended for assessment under the *Code of Practice* for a statement of special educational needs at the pre-school stage as their needs usually become more apparent when they start full-time education. If parents have concerns, they may ask the LA to make a statutory assessment. The LA then decides whether or not such an assessment is necessary. If the LA decides that it is not necessary, the LA writes and tells the parents (normally within six weeks) the reasons for this decision. Parents may appeal to the Special Educational Needs Tribunal if they disagree with the decision. Further details are given in the next section, 'Assessment at school age'. In the US the assessment procedure is the same for pre-school and school-aged children. The children are assessed under the Individuals with Disabilities Education Act (IDEA). The parents or the school can request an initial evaluation.

The Department for Education and Skills publishes a very useful leaflet, *Special Educational Needs (SEN) – a Guide for Parents and Carers* (DfES 2001b), which should be given to parents by the LA if a statutory assessment is to be carried out. A useful leaflet for parents in the US is *Communicating with Your Child's School Through Letter Writing: A Parent's Guide* (Rebhorn and Kupper 2002). This is available from the National Dissemination Center for Children with Disabilities (NICHCY) and can be downloaded from their website, www.nichcy.org. For details of how to obtain copies of these documents see Appendix 1.

All schools and early years settings in the UK should now have a written SEN policy that parents can request to see.

ASSESSMENT AT SCHOOL AGE

When a child is identified as having special educational needs by his school, the school must carry out a similar procedure to above going through the graduated response of School Action and School Action Plus initially as set out in the *SEN Code of Practice*. See section 'Assesment in the US' below.

School Action

When the school has identified a child with special educational needs then they should put into place appropriate interventions to support the child. These should be additional or different from what normally happens for pupils with no SEN but provided from within the school's own resources. Similarly to Early Years Action, an IEP must be drawn up to support the child and parents must be fully informed and consulted. Other professionals who may be already involved such as therapists should also be consulted with parental agreement.

School Action Plus

The decision to move from School Action to School Action Plus is likely to be taken at an IEP review meeting organized by the SENCO with the child's parents and teacher present. Other professionals would also be consulted at this point. The reasons for the move to School Action Plus are likely to be lack of progress or if the child is working well below the level of other pupils. Also the pupil may have a sensory, physical or emotional need and may require specialist support or equipment.

Statutory assessment

In the same way as for a child at Early Years Action Plus, the school must identify that the child has 'demonstrated a significant cause for concern' (DfES 2001a, p.56). The usual routes for starting the statutory assessment procedure is following a referral by the child's school, pre-school or parent. Occasionally referrals can be made by representatives of the social services or health departments such as a therapist, paediatrician or social worker. If the referral is not being made directly by a parent, then parents should be consulted before requesting an assessment. If a parent or school requests assessment and the LA does not agree, they have the right to appeal. At the time of request the school or pre-school must provide evidence obtained during Early Years Action, Early Years Action Plus, School Action and School Action Plus including the views of parents, the child (where possible and appropriate), copies of the IEP, details of progress and other evidence including the advice of other professionals involved.

There are specific guidelines on the timetable for assessment. The LA must make a decision on whether or not to assess within six weeks of the request for assessment. Following this request the LA will formally notify the parents and give information on all the timescales and give the parents the name of the person they should contact if they have any queries, i.e. 'the Named Officer'. They will ask parents to provide evidence, which can be written or spoken, giving reasons why the child should be assessed. Parents have at least 29 days to send this to the LA. Parents should also be informed about the LA's Parent Partnership Service which can provide independent help and support throughout the process.

By the end of the initial six weeks the LA must inform parents whether they are going to carry out an assessment. Parents can ask the Named Person to explain any delay and consult with the Parent Partnership Service. As a last resort the parent can complain to the Secretary of State for Children, Schools and Families. If the LA decides not to assess a child, the parent has the right to appeal to the Special Educational Needs Tribunal. If there are unreasonable delays in the statutory assessment process the parent can complain to the Local Government Ombudsman

The assessment is carried out next and the LA will ask advice from a range of professionals involved with the child, such as the school or pre-school teachers, educational psychologist, doctor or paediatrician, physiotherapist, speech and language therapist, occupational therapist and social services department. Parents will be asked for their views again at this stage and can suggest any other specialists or experts who they would like involved in the assessment. This part of the assessment should take no longer than a further ten weeks. The LA then has two weeks to consider the assessments and make a decision. If they decide to make a statement of special educational needs for the child, they will send the parents a copy of the proposed or draft statement to read. Parents are asked to give their views and need to inform the LA at this stage if they are not happy with any aspect of the statement. If the LA decides not to issue a proposed statement, the parents will be notified of the decision. At this stage the parent again has the right of appeal to the Special Educational Needs Tribunal.

The proposed statement does not include details of type of school. Parents have 15 days to comment on the proposed statement and to say which school they prefer (which may be the child's current school). The final statement is usually made within eight weeks of the proposed statement and will include details of the school suggested by the LA. The whole statutory assessment procedure should be normally completed within six months.

The final statement will have details of the child's needs and the provision that will be made to address these needs. The child's IEP will normally be reviewed within two months and a full review of his needs will be carried out every twelve months. Parents will be fully involved in annual review meetings. During these meetings the statement will be reviewed, the progress the child has made towards the objectives set will be discussed, and new targets set for the following year. There is a general move to include pupils more in the annual review procedure; at the very least the pupils' views should be represented. Person-centred reviews were initially developed in schools to support the Year 9 transition review in schools. Pupils at this time will be around the age of 13 or 14 years old and a transition review is for the pupil and everyone involved to look ahead to what the pupil will be doing in the future with regard to education and what choices are available. Bailey *et al.* (2009) give details of Ellen Tinkham School, an all-age special school in Devon which has successfully used this type of review with all its pupils. Person-centred reviews are based on person-centred thinking tools, which have been developed by the Learning Community for Person Centred Practices (www.learningcommunity.us).

ASSESSMENT IN THE US

There are ten steps in the assessment procedure under the Individuals with Disabilities Education Act (IDEA).

1. *Identification*

    The parents or the child's school can make a request for evaluation. Parental consent is needed to proceed to step 2.

2. *Evaluation*

    Evaluation needs to be completed within 60 days of the parents giving consent. Following the evaluation the results will be used to decide on an appropriate educational programme for the child.

3. *Eligibility is decided*

    The parents and a group of relevant professionals look at the evaluation results to determine eligibility. If parents disagree with the evaluation results then they may request an Independent Educational Evaluation (IEE). Parents may also request a hearing to challenge the evaluation.

4. *Child eligible for services*
   If the child is eligible for special education and related services then within 30 calendar days the IEP team must meet to write an Individualized Educational Program (IEP) for the child.

5. *IEP meeting*
   This is organised by the school system and relevant professionals including the parents are invited. Parents may also invite people to the meeting with knowledge or special expertise about their child.

6. *The IEP is written*
   During the IEP meeting the IEP is written. If appropriate the student may be included at the meeting as part of the IEP team. The parents must consent to any special education or related services provision. If the parents disagree then they can ask for mediation. They may also file a complaint with the state education agency and request a due process hearing.

7. *Provision*
   The school must ensure that services are provided as detailed in the IEP.

8. *Progress review*
   The child's progress is measured towards the annual goals stated on the IEP. Parents will be regularly informed of their child's progress towards their goals during the school year.

9. *IEP review*
   The IEP is reviewed at least once a year by the IEP team. Parents can request a review earlier. Parents must be invited to the review and can make suggestions for change and express their agreement or disagreement on the child's IEP goals or placement.

10. *Re-evaluation*
    The child must be re-evaluated at least every three years unless the parents and school agree this is not necessary. This re-evaluation is sometimes called a triennial.

ASSESSMENTS BY SPECIALISTS
Physiotherapy and occupational therapy assessment
The physiotherapist and the occupational therapist may be asked to assess children individually or as part of a multidisciplinary assessment – they may well carry out a joint assessment. Referrals may be made by the child's

general practitioner (GP), paediatrician or the school medical officer. Referrals may also be made by educational psychologists, social workers or the headteacher. Referral procedures vary depending on the area, and there may well be waiting lists for assessment. These assessments may be carried out as part of the statutory assessment described above or as the result of a general concern expressed by the parents or by the medical practitioner. In the US, referrals to therapists are part of the assessment procedure as part of the IEP and come under the term 'related services'. For children who have not been assessed under IDEA referrals may be made by their family medical practitioner.

Normally the physiotherapist will assess gross motor coordination. An assessment tool frequently used by physiotherapists is the Movement Assessment Battery for Children (Movement ABC-2) (Henderson and Sugden 2007), which was mentioned in Chapter 1.

The occupational therapist will assess fine motor coordination which includes, depending on the age of the child, looking at his pencil skills with regard to writing or drawing. Other areas which may be assessed by the occupational therapist are visual-perceptual skills, tactile discrimination and daily-living skills such as dressing and eating, particularly if there are concerns in these areas.

The assessment may include standardized tests and qualitative observations. The therapist will complete a report following the assessment and suggest an appropriate plan of action. This plan may include individual or group therapy sessions, advice for the school and programmes to carry out in the home.

The physiotherapist may advise the school on activities for physical education which will help ensure that the child is included in PE as much as possible. Advice from the occupational therapist for the school may include pre-writing or handwriting exercises, recommendations on seating and on the positioning of writing (involving, for instance, a sloping board) and on drawing materials such as suitable pens or pencils or pencil grips. The therapist may advise on strategies to help the child master dressing skills; she may give a task analysis of a difficult skill such as tying laces. Advice may also be given on how to help the child overcome difficulties with eating meals – special non-slip mats or cutlery may be advised if necessary.

Speech and language therapy assessment

Speech and language therapists use a variety of standardized and non-standardized assessment tools. Information will be gathered from the parents regarding any feeding, swallowing, eating or drinking difficulties, as well as details about the child's understanding and his expressive language. From this information his developmental levels will be assessed. If appropriate, standardized assessments of receptive and expressive language will be carried out.

Other areas assessed by the speech and language therapist may include:

- Production of speech sounds and the sequencing of sounds including words in sentences.

- Pragmatic skills (social communication) including the understanding of 'hidden meanings' (e.g. sarcasm, idioms, the importance of stress and intonation). The speech and language therapist may ask the parents and school to complete a questionnaire to help assess pragmatic skills.

- Oral skills, which include the voluntary control of lips, tongue, jaw, the soft palate and other muscles of the mouth; and assessment of whether the child has a saliva-control problem. Also included is breath control as this affects speech – it may be 'breathy', or come in a rush – and quality of speech (e.g. whether the child's speech is too loud or too soft, the pitch of the voice and the intonation).

- Non-verbal methods of communication (e.g. the use of gesture, eye contact, facial expression).

The educational psychologist's assessment

Shapiro (1991, p.4) advises that 'before treatment is suggested, it is important for the child to have a full psychological assessment so that his particular cognitive pattern can be evaluated'. In most cases the child will be seen by the educational psychologist as part of the statutory assessment procedure described earlier in this chapter. This may take the form of standardized tests and/or qualitative observation and information gathered from teachers and parents. The child's performance with regard to the National Curriculum will also be taken into account, including any difficulties he has in accessing the curriculum (e.g. because of motor difficulties he may find it hard to record written work). In the US the curriculum is not standardised at a national level. The No Child Left Behind Act allows each state to formulate their own curriculum under certain limitations. The educational or school psychologist would discuss the child's progress with their teacher to assess whether it is within normal grade levels for his age.

Portwood (1996, 1999), a senior educational psychologist, describes a series of assessments she has carried out to assess children with dyspraxia. Information collected would include background information on the family such as the number of children; the age of the mother; details of the pregnancy; birth details; the child's developmental profile including motor, social and language skills. The Wechsler Intelligence Scale for Children (WISC-III) (Wechsler 1992) would be carried out with children aged six years and older, along with a motor-skills screening test. With older children details would also be obtained of reading and spelling ages along with numeracy attainments and perceptual skills.

The WISC-III is a commonly used cognitive measure. Portwood (1998) says that often discrepancies between verbal and performance scores are used to diagnose dyspraxia, where the verbal score is significantly higher than the performance score. She considers that it is 'unhelpful to give the accumulative scores for verbal and performance IQ because that disguises the particular strengths in the child's cognitive profile' (Portwood 1998, p.14). The individual scores for the sub-tests which make up the two main sections – performance and verbal skills – should be viewed as a profile giving information on the child's abilities. The sub-tests which comprise the verbal scores give scores on information (general knowledge), similarities (why two words are similar), arithmetic, vocabulary, comprehension and digit span (repeating a series of numbers). The performance scores combine sub-test scores on picture completion, coding (copying symbols by drawing), picture arrangement (sequencing pictures in the correct order), block design (copying a two-dimensional pattern using cubes) and object assembly. Portwood considers that 'If the scaled scores in the sub-tests of arithmetic, digit span, coding and block design are significantly depressed in relation to the other scores, these are indications that the child is dyspraxic' (Portwood 1998, p.15).

The educational psychologist is often the professional who gathers all the evidence together from the various sources such as the parents, teachers and other professionals. She is instrumental in drawing up intervention strategies and coordinating them. The educational psychologist may offer specific advice on teaching programmes or be able to give parents information on support groups. She will also take the views of the child into account.

The class teacher and/or SENCO's assessment

Nash-Wortham and Hunt (1997) give a simple method of assessment which can be carried out by teachers using six 'pointers'. These pointers do not assess whether or not a child has dyspraxia but give clear guidance on which areas he is experiencing difficulty. The six pointers are:

- Timing and rhythm.

- Direction and goal (e.g. left, right, in relation to turning, pointing or movement).

- Sequencing (verbal and motor sequencing).

- Fine motor control for speech, writing and reading.

- Laterality (whether a child has cross-laterality, i.e. mixed dominance, such as being right-footed and left-handed).

- Spatial orientation and movement.

Nash-Wortham and Hunt (1997) then give a series of exercises to address each of the six pointers. The exercises are clearly described and simple to carry out.

COMMONLY USED ASSESSMENT TOOLS
The following tools are commonly used in the UK and US.

Movement Assessment Battery for Children (Movement ABC-2)
As mentioned above, the Movement ABC-2 is used with children who have movement difficulties. It can be used for the assessment of children aged 3 to 16 years.

Test scores assess gross and fine motor skills in three areas:

- Manual dexterity.

- Ball skills.

- Static and dynamic balance.

The test also involves:

- Qualitative observations on the three above areas.

- Assessment of influences on performance (i.e. Is the child observed to be overactive, passive, timid, tense, impulsive, distractible, disorganized or confused? Does he overestimate or underestimate his own ability, lack persistence, get upset by failure, appear to get no pleasure from success?).

- Assessment of physical factors (i.e. weight, height, weight in relation to height, vision, hearing, speech, anatomical or postural defects).

The test employs percentile scores. Children who score between the fifth and fifteenth percentile can be considered to have a degree of difficulty that is borderline. Opportunities for the practice of skills at school and home will usually be recommended. A score below the fifth percentile indicates that the child has a motor difficulty which requires intervention, such as a management or remediation programme. Scoring on or below the fifth percentile means that the child falls into the bottom 5 per cent of the population in terms of motor skills.

Test of Visual-Perceptual Skills (non-motor) (TVPS)

The purpose of the TVPS is to determine a child's visual-perceptual strengths and weaknesses on the basis of non-motor visual-perceptual testing (Gardner 1982). Visual perception is the ability to use visual information to recognize, recall, discriminate and make meaning of what we see.

This test comprises seven areas of visual-perceptual skills; it shows how a child perceives various forms (black outline figures of two-dimensional abstract shapes, both familiar and unfamiliar) and the way these forms can be interpreted. The results indicate the likelihood of difficulties with schoolwork with regard to these areas, as follows.

VISUAL DISCRIMINATION

Difficulties with visual discrimination indicate that the child may have problems with the recognition of words, letters and numbers. He may find categorization difficult, such as recognizing similarities and differences in letter formation and patterns in the spelling of words. Matching words, pictures, letters, numbers and quantities of objects may cause difficulties too.

VISUAL MEMORY

Difficulties with visual memory may affect immediate and delayed recall of material when reading flashcards of letters, words and sentences, when reading words in books, and in remembering the form of letters when writing them.

VISUAL-SPATIAL RELATIONSHIPS

Difficulties with visual-spatial relationships may mean that the child has trouble writing words and letters on lines. He may reverse letters, numbers and words. Keeping neat margins and spacing between words and setting out maths problems may also be hard for him.

VISUAL FORM CONSTANCY

Difficulties with visual form constancy mean that it is more difficult to match letters and shapes and to recognize words out of a familiar context (e.g. if written in a different size, print or colour than usual).

VISUAL SEQUENTIAL MEMORY

Difficulties with visual sequential memory mean that the child may find it hard to sequence letters in a given order, which may lead to difficulties in reading and spelling.

VISUAL FIGURE-GROUND DISCRIMINATION

Difficulties in visual figure-ground discrimination mean that it is hard for him to see detail in pictures or text, and this may lead to difficulties in copying from the blackboard or from a written text or when transferring written material to a computer. The child may find it difficult to keep his place and know where he is when copying and so may miss out chunks of work.

VISUAL CLOSURE

Difficulties with visual closure can involve problems with recognizing an individual letter, word or object from a partial presentation of its form. This will affect speed of accurate reading, the ability to study quickly a visual presentation such as a map or chart, and the ability to develop study skills in the older child such as speed-reading and scanning.

This test can be used to give a profile of a child's performance within the seven areas of visual-perceptual skills. It is used to gain information on the areas of weakness which may have an influence on his handwriting abilities.

Goodenough Draw-a-Man Test

This test was developed by Florence Goodenough in 1926 and revised in 1963. It includes three drawings that the child is asked to make – of a man, a woman and the child's drawing of himself (Harris 1963). The test can be used with children aged 4 to 12 years. It was originally designed as a measure of intelligence but is still sometimes used as a screening measure to evaluate conceptual maturity and to give an indication of intellectual functioning. This raw score needs to be used with caution because 9 out of the 50 items need lines to be 'firm and meeting' or 'attached' or 'continuous', and the ability to score on these items could be affected by motor difficulties, which may or may not be related to intellectual functioning.

Developmental Test of Visual-Motor Integration (VMI)

The VMI is appropriate for children aged 2 to 18 years (Beery and Buktenica 2004). Research has shown that the VMI used alongside other tests has predicted which children are likely to have reading difficulties. Predictive correlations decline as children get older, which is presumed to be due to their developing compensatory skills.

The test consists of the child using a pencil to copy a developmental sequence of 21 or 30 geometric forms. The ability to copy geometric forms is related to the skills needed in maths and handwriting. This test can also be used with children who have handwriting problems, with a view to advising on whether an individual's difficulties may be related to visual-motor integration.

Test of Auditory-Perceptual Skills Revised (TAPS-R)

The TAPS-R (Gardner 1996) is used to assess the following auditory perceptual skills:

- auditory number memory (forward and backward)

- auditory sentence memory

- auditory word memory

- auditory interpretation of directions

- auditory word discrimination

- auditory processing (thinking and reasoning).

There is also a parent's questionnaire for parents to give information on their child's skills. The results give a profile of auditory-perceptual skills. The age range is from 4 to 12 years.

Observations of locomotor skills, posture, tone and stability

Aspects observed can include hopping, moving in a wheelbarrow position, stability in kneeling positions and strength in supine and prone positions. Skills such as walking on the heels and on different edges of the feet can be observed, and any associated reactions with the hands.

Observations of handwriting or computer use

The child can be asked to write his name, copy a simple phrase such as 'a big red bus' and individual letters and numerals. The writing is examined for the following points: consistency of the size of the letters, whether joined script is used, the slope of the letters, orientation to the line the child is writing on, and the spacing between letters and words. His hand and eye dominance is noted. Also observed is the type of grip the child uses to hold his pencil, and whether undue pressure is used. The therapist will also note his seating posture and the use of his non-dominant hand.

If computer use is being looked at, details will be taken of the child's home or school equipment. His use of mouse, roller-ball and keyboard and his seating position relative to the keyboard and screen will be examined.

Other observations related to organizational skills

Other observations may include asking the child to remember a short shopping list of articles and asking him to carry out a sequence of actions from memory.

A GENERAL WORD ABOUT ASSESSMENTS

Assessments need to be carried out in a reasonably short time – children get tired if the session is too long. After the assessment, practical advice should be given as soon as possible. If a child is statemented, the statement of special educational needs should include advice and recommendations and be circulated to all relevant persons. The parents, the school, the therapists, the social services department (if relevant) and any other agencies involved, as well as the child, should know what has been recommended. If the relevant people are not informed about the assessment and the recommended programme, it will not be carried out to its full extent and will consequently be less effective. For details about US equivalents please see section 'Assessment in the US' above.

Assessment procedure used at Vranch House

It may be of interest to readers to hear of the procedure carried out at Vranch House.

SCREENING

Devon LA, like several other local authorities in the UK, is planning to introduce a programme in all schools to enable identification of children with movement difficulties and give early intervention by school staff. One programme used by a number of Devon schools is BEAM (Balance Education and Movement) which was originally developed in south-east England (Finlayson and Rickard 2001). Only pupils with more severe difficulties would be referred for therapy following a one-term intervention programme by the schools. There is a number of other assessment and intervention tools such as Fun Fit in Cornwall (see Appendix 2) and some health authority areas are developing their own screening programmes for schools to use.

ASSESSMENT

Following referral a request will be made for a report from the child's present school giving details of the following:

- Physical gross motor skills – climbing stairs, balance, coordination, ball skills, running swimming, use of playground/gym equipment.

- Activities involving fine motor skills – handwriting, use of scissors, ICT/mouse skills, copying from the board.

- Functional skills – for example dressing for PE, self-care.

- Understanding instructions, concentration and attention.

- Organizational skills.

- Academic level compared with peers.

- Self-esteem, behaviour and social skills.

Parents are also asked to complete a questionnaire covering similar areas to the above with relevant medical information and details of the child's interests and skills.

The team consisting of a physiotherapist and an occupational therapist will then examine the reports and carry out an assessment if appropriate. The criteria for assessment are that the child's main difficulty is with gross or fine motor skills.

If the child has both gross motor and fine motor difficulties, he will have assessments carried out by the physiotherapist and occupational therapist. If he has only fine motor difficulties, the assessment will be with the occupational therapist and similarly if he has only gross motor difficulties with the physiotherapist. The child and his parents will be invited for an appointment that will last about an hour. Sometimes the child's learning support assistant from his school will be invited to attend, providing the parents agree. The family is made welcome and the assessment procedure is explained to them by the therapist. Initially the therapist will ask the child some simple questions to make him feel at home, such as his name, his school and which activities he does or does not enjoy. During the assessment the child and his parents will be asked what is most important for them, for example problems with PE (which could indicate poor core stability), brushing teeth (self-care) or organizational skills.

Some standardized measures are used judiciously depending on the child's needs.

AFTER THE ASSESSMENT

Clear SMART goals will be identified and often a sticker chart for motivation is given with the agreement of the child and parents. A written report of the findings and recommendations is provided for parents and all relevant agencies. Following the assessment the child may be given advice and an individual written programme to do at home and school or be offered a place in a group held at Vranch House.

At the time of writing the criteria for a child to attend a group for regular therapy would be as follows.

Gross and fine motor group

- Full prior assessment by physiotherapist and/or occupational therapist.

- Potential for improved gross and fine motor skills (usually a six-week programme).

- Self-esteem possibly at risk.

- Aged between six and eight years and attending mainstream school.

- Would benefit from group activities.

Fine motor group

- Attending mainstream school.

- Prior assessment by physiotherapist and/or occupational therapist.

- Difficulties with handwriting/fine motor skills.

- Self-esteem possibly at risk.

- Aged 6–11 (there are different levels to suit differing ability ranges).

An information leaflet and programme is given to parents and carers (Vranch House 2009).

A personal experience of assessment and support at Vranch House

Mark had an initial assessment when he first started school at four or five years of age. He had seen the same therapist periodically over the past six years and initially attended the gross motor group and then the fine motor group specifically for handwriting skills. Each group lasted for half a term (six or seven weeks) and Mark attended once a week initially for an hour and a half and later for an hour a week.

Mark's mother said, 'It's quite intense, what they do, but quite good fun. At the end you go to see what they've achieved. They get set homework – practising patterns and that. Mark used to master some quite difficult patterns.'

Mark's therapist also did an outreach programme at his primary school to give advice to staff on handwriting and fine motor control.

Chapter 6

INTERVENTIONS IN SCHOOL

Primary or Elementary School

THE CLASS TEACHER'S PERSPECTIVE

Perhaps a child in your class has been identified as having dyspraxia. You already knew he had special educational needs long before all the specialists were involved; in fact, you may have been the person to bring his difficulties to the attention of the SENCO (special education teacher/educator in the US) and the parents. Depending on which stage of the *Code of Practice* he has been assessed to, you may or may not have a statement. If you and your SENCO wrote his individual education plan at School Action stage, you still may not be sure how to meet his movement needs as you have had no specialist advice. Alternatively you may have received reports with suggestions from the child's educational psychologist, physiotherapist, occupational therapist, speech and language therapist or other specialist support agency. They may have given you special programmes of work to carry out. The child may attend a special centre for therapy and you may have been given the name of a person to contact at that centre. It can be confusing and frustrating because you have many other children in the class with varying needs and the pressure of the literacy and numeracy framework (Reading First or Early Readers in the US), along with all the other initiatives that seem to arrive on your desk daily such as AFL (Assessment For Learning), APP (Assessing Pupils' Progress), citizenship and SEAL (Social and Emotional Aspects of Learning) to name but a few! US initiatives include No Child Left Behind (NCLB) and Healthier School Challenge. You may have a couple of hours' learning support assistant time for the child if you are lucky. If you work in the US then you may have been involved in identifying the child as needing special education and related services. You may have discussed this with the parents and your principal and been involved in an IEP meeting and writing his IEP under IDEA.

UK documents

I would advise class teachers to make sure they have the following documents or information:

- If the child does not have a statement, check with your headteacher and SENCO to see if any *specialist reports* have been received from therapists, educational psychologists or others.

- Statement of special educational needs (if appropriate).

- Annual review reports.

- The child's individual education plan.

- Reports from specialists that have been issued since the statement.

STATEMENT OF SPECIAL EDUCATIONAL NEEDS (IF APPROPRIATE)

Check that you have all the appendices as well. These are the detailed reports from the educational psychologist, school medical officer and other agencies such as the social services department. Parents' letters and submissions will also be included. The school medical officer's appendix may contain reports from a physiotherapist, a speech and language therapist, an occupational therapist or other medical specialists. The occupational therapist's report may be in the appendix from the social services department, as many of them are employed as community occupational therapists and work directly for the local social services department alongside social workers. If a child has a care manager this person may be a social worker or a community occupational therapist. The appendices may not be with the final statement because they are usually sent out with the proposed statement, so you may have to request these from your SENCO or the Education Office.

ANNUAL REVIEW REPORTS

If the statement is over a year old, check to see you have these. If you do not have copies, check with your SENCO.

- The *names and telephone numbers of any therapists* currently working with the child – if you do not know who is involved the parents should be able to tell you, or telephone the centre the child attends and ask. Make sure you talk to the person concerned and invite him or her to come out and meet you at school.

THE CHILD'S INDIVIDUAL EDUCATION PLAN

If you were involved at School Action stage you should have this, but if the child has changed classes or even schools since then, chase it up. Your SEN-CO should have it if you do not have a copy. You will be directly involved in updating the IEP which should be done at least every six months.

REPORTS FROM SPECIALISTS THAT HAVE BEEN ISSUED SINCE THE STATEMENT

Check with your head teacher and SENCO for any such reports.

US documents

- Initial evaluation reports. These are from the initial multidisciplinary assessment which will have included relevant therapists, specialist teachers, school psychologist and medical specialists. The parents may have also requested an Independent Educational Evaluation (IEE).

- Individualized educational program (IEP). This will have been agreed by the IEP team at the IEP meeting.

- Progress reports. Parents should be sent regular progress reports towards the child's annual goals on their IEP.

- IEP reviews. The review should be carried out at least once a year involving a team of professionals working with the child and their parents.

- Re-evaluation reports (where appropriate). Re-evaluations are carried out every three years unless the parents and school agree that this is not necessary.

THE PARENTS' PERSPECTIVE

As parents you are likely to have been aware that there were difficulties long before the school mentioned it to you. You may have expressed your anxieties at an early stage in your child's development or education; perhaps these were brushed aside and you were told that he is just 'a late developer'. You may have been instrumental in getting him a statement of special educational needs.

Make sure of the following points.

In the UK

- If your child has a statement of special educational needs, this should be subject to an annual review – the first one will usually be due a year after the date of the final statement. This will normally comprise the headteacher or SENCO gathering reports from all relevant persons, including yourselves, and holding a meeting to which you and others are invited to review your child's statement. Do check that this review happens – in some very small rural primary schools, when a child is the first there with a statement, the headteacher may be unfamiliar with the procedure.

- Your child should have an individual education plan if he has been assessed to at least the School Action stage of the *Code of Practice*. This should be reviewed by the school regularly.

- Liaise with the school so that you can support the IEP targets at home where appropriate. Your child should also be aware of the targets he is working towards. The targets should be realistically achievable within, for example, a term or six months.

In the US

- If your child has an individualized educational program (IEP) then you should be sent regular reports on your child's progress towards their annual goals.

- A full IEP review and meeting should be carried out at least once a year. If you have concerns you can request an earlier review. You can make suggestions for changes at this meeting if you feel it is necessary. If you do not agree with the goals set or provision decided you can make your concerns known at this meeting.

- At least every three years your child must re-evaluated unless you and the school agree that this is not necessary. This is called a 'triennial evaluation'. At this time your child is re-assessed to confirm that he is still 'a child with a disability' and what his educational needs are under the Individuals with Disabilities Education Act (IDEA). You have the right to request a new evaluation if you feel this is necessary at any other time.

In the UK and the US

- Liaise with any other professionals providing support for your child – for example, the physiotherapist, the occupational therapist or speech and language therapist. If they are providing individual or group therapy sessions, be aware of what areas they are working on and make sure your child's school knows about this extra support.

- If your child receives extra time from a teaching/teacher assistant or learning support assistant, find out his or her name. He or she may well be the person who gets to know your child best in school and who sees where problems develop before even the class teacher.

- If your child seems worried, unhappy or reluctant to go to school, talk to the class teacher. Remember – you know your child best.

ADVICE TO PARENTS

Mark's mother said:

> One thing I found very hard when Mark started at primary school was that he couldn't write his own name and I knew then there was something not right. It isn't until your child starts to read it becomes more obvious and when he was in Year 1 or Year 2 it sort of highlighted it.[1] If I knew then what I know now I think I'd be a lot more keyed up, it took so long. I remember he got assessed by an educational psychologist that showed he was well behind with his reading and writing and certain things he wasn't too bad on. After about a year I began to get very cross that nothing was being done about it. I couldn't understand this educational psychologist not saying what was wrong with my child. I did tell him straight, 'You will not label my child because as soon as you label him you know that you've got to come forward with the money to help him.' I was getting very cross with the whole system and then after a while the school decided to get the educational psychologist back in again and they suggested applying for a statement for Mark. But by the time we got the statement in place he was in Year 5 and I just thought of all the time he hadn't been getting any extra help in school. I think parents need to be made much more aware of the way the system works. I felt way out of my depth. I'm not stupid

---

1   Year 1 is the second year the child is in school when they are aged between five and six years old. Year 2 is the third year in school.

by any means – I'm active in the family business, I'm the director of a company – but I found it really hard. I felt like I needed some sort of qualification in the law to get through it.

Mark's mother got support from the Parent Partnership Service, who supported her in attending a meeting and giving advice on the statementing procedure, which was very helpful. Even with this support it was still difficult although she was successful in achieving what she wanted for her son in the end.

> I found it a total battle. I'd get very cross and upset and then I'd go into these meetings all guns blazing and say this is what I want, I'm not accepting anything less. It worked because the amount of support went from 0.3 to 0.5 on his statement.[2] I told them that I wanted 0.7 but my aim was to get him 0.5. I couldn't see myself getting any more than that.
>
> From then Mark has had 0.5 support. The school had some problems initially finding people who would stay. One person just left without warning and the next person had to move due to personal circumstances. Fortunately the last person was with him throughout Year 6.
>
> I think if parents have got any concerns with their child they should go to the GP. It's difficult to know who to go to. You can talk to the teachers but the only way you're going to get any help is by going to your GP and getting referred to a paediatrician. My GP was very understanding because he's got children of his own with difficulties. He knew exactly where I was coming from and knew exactly what to do. I think I was just very, very lucky that he knew who to contact. 'You need to see the paediatrician' he said and wrote to him straight away. The GP referred Mark to Vranch House for therapy at the same time.

SATS

One of the biggest problems that the dyspraxic child faces at primary school is the standard assessment tests (SATs), which happen at the end of Year 6 when children are 10 or 11 years old. Mark was given extra time for his papers. The tests were in three subjects – English, mathematics and science.[3]

---

2   For example 0.5 support refers to a child having a teaching assistant working with him for half the school week overall; 0.8 would be 80 per cent of the time.

3   Since 2010 the science papers have been discontinued.

For the science and maths tests Mark was allowed to have a reader (amanuensis). Mark passed his science and maths tests with a good grade (level 4) – the highest grade being level 5. His English tests were more problematic. If the school judges that a child is below level 3 then they do not need to enter the child for the test. Instead his teacher can assess his level within the school setting. His mother said, 'With the English test they wouldn't allow him to sit it properly to start with. So I wrote off to all different people and in the end they agreed he could sit it at the same time as the others but he didn't get marked as such.'

Mark and his mother had spent a great deal of time preparing him for the English test. She said:

> He can still comprehend English although he can't write it down and he can't read it. Somebody can read him a passage out, read him a question and he can answer it – that's what I was doing at home, I don't see why it still couldn't stand as something. I wanted him to feel the same as his peers. It was unfair to say that he wasn't going to sit it at all.

PRACTICAL ADVICE FOR THE CLASS TEACHER AND TEACHING/LEARNING SUPPORT ASSISTANTS
Handwriting and fine motor activities

Ensure that the child is sitting properly, as poor posture can have an enormous effect on handwriting or other fine motor skills. Even reading a book can be difficult if the child is wriggling around and has his head too close to or too far away from the book. These are the basic points to bear in mind:

- The child should be sitting with his feet flat on the floor. His bottom should be well back on the seat and his overall posture should be symmetrical. His head should be in midline (i.e. in line with the centre of his body and symmetrical on his shoulders). He may find it much easier to write on a surface that is sloping slightly upwards. Special boards can be purchased or, alternatively, a large A4 file placed so that the spine is furthest away from him may well be sufficient.

- If the occupational therapist has advised on a special pen or pencil grip, ensure the child uses it. Special triangular pencils may also be advised, to encourage him to use a tripod grip.

- Check the child's pencil pressure. If he is pressing too hard, his writing will be distorted and he will quickly become fatigued. Encourage a comfortable, effective pencil grip.

- The most appropriate paper position may not be square on the table but slightly angled.

- A labelled pencil case is a good idea, to keep his things together, as he may well mislay this item from time to time. Spares can be kept by his teaching/learning support assistant or teacher and returned to that person at the end of the lesson.

- Non-slip mats such as the Dycem range are a good idea for fixing all sorts of things to the table such as sorting trays, paint pots or exercise or reading books. These mats can be rinsed out quickly when they lose their power to stick and returned to their original condition. Dycem can also be bought in rolls and appropriate lengths can be cut off (see Appendix 1 for details).

- Soft plastic reusable adhesive putty offers another useful way of fixing things, so make sure he has some in his pencil case.

- Handwriting practice sheets are helpful, as they give the child a model to start from and clear indications of where to start on the page. Having just a blank sheet of paper and being expected to copy off the blackboard or whiteboard may give him enormous difficulties. He may have to draw lines with a ruler first, and get them the right distance apart, before he can even work out where to start writing.

- Many children with movement difficulties find it easier to develop cursive handwriting rather than writing individual print-style letters. Many of the published handwriting schemes contain photocopy masters which encourage the development of flow in writing.

Rosemary Sassoon (1998, p.38) gives five essential rules of handwriting:

1. Our writing goes from left to right and top to bottom.

2. Each letter has a conventional point of entry and direction of stroke.

3. Letters have different heights.

4. Letters and words need to be spaced appropriately.

5. Capital letters and small letters are different and have different uses.

English and mathematics

One common problem is setting out work, particularly when writing or doing maths. Worksheets can be very helpful if they are simple and easy to follow. The aim of the maths lesson may, for example, be to practise addition of numbers over 100. Unfortunately, the child may spend most of the lesson setting out the problems, then adding the wrong numbers because the columns are not aligned. When writing, pre-lined paper may help but make sure that the lines are not too close together – give the child space to write.

Another confusion experienced by dyspraxic children is that in reading and writing they are told to go from left to right, but in setting out mathematical problems they have to work from right to left. It is useful to discuss this with the children because they may never have realized the difference, and the awareness of this will help them to understand why they have been getting it wrong.

Often, for young children literacy and numeracy sessions and other activities such as circle time and story time involve sitting on a carpet or on the floor. This is a difficult seating position for dyspraxic children, who may fidget a lot and become an irritation to their neighbours. If there is alternative seating such as classroom chairs, the difficulty may be overcome, although this has to be done sensitively so that the dyspraxic child is not singled out.

Physical education

PE is one of the dyspraxic child's most challenging activities. If he manages to avoid physical activities because of fear of failure, he will become less fit and the situation will get worse. O'Beirne, Larkin and Cable (1994) in a study of coordination problems and anaerobic performance found that children who were poorly coordinated were significantly less fit. Fitness is an issue in schools at the present time because the modern child spends more time pursuing sedentary leisure activities such as watching television or playing computer or playstation games.

The National Curriculum for physical education stresses the importance of inclusive PE. The Youth Sports Trust also provides a resource on its website to help teachers, parents and coaches promote inclusive PE. These include the TOP programmes which are designed as an inclusive PE resource. In the US the National Association for Sport and Education website (see Appendix 2) is a useful resource for teachers and parents, including lots of good ideas, and a useful download called Teacher's Toolbox, which has many ideas about physical activities. Also the Let's Move website (see

Appendix 1) offers tips for improving children's fitness. See Appendix 1 for details of the National Curriculum for PE and Appendix 2 for the Youth Sports Trust.

The suggestions for PE in the following section are specifically for the dyspraxic child, but will be useful for many other children with a range of special needs and for young children generally:

- Make sure all instructions are clear and simple, and that everyone hears them.

- If the children are in groups and going round a circuit in the playground, hall or gymnasium, be sure to provide a simpler alternative to any activities that are obviously going to be too difficult for the dyspraxic child. For instance:

  o Ensure that climbing equipment has two routes, one higher and one much nearer the ground.

  o With bat-and-ball activities ensure a range of equipment which includes lightweight large-headed bats with short handles, and larger foam balls.

  o With aiming activities such as skittles or other target games, ensure that if balls are used, beanbags are also available. Larger targets will help as well.

- Make use of 'Beat your own record' activities. Children try to catch, bounce or jump more times in a minute than they did on the previous occasion. The use of the question, 'How many of you beat your own record?' offers a chance for the dyspraxic child to succeed even though his total may be lower than that of many other children. The teaching/learning support assistant can help him to count and keep a record if necessary.

- Circular non-slip mats or 'spots' are very helpful in a gymnastics lesson to help children to return to a 'space' in the hall or gymnasium. The action, by the whole class, of placing spots and then moving off and returning to a spot is a useful activity in itself. It also ensures that the dyspraxic child has a place to aim for and is not getting in anyone's way. Small gym mats are also useful in helping children stay in their own space.

- Non-competitive activities such as individual gymnastics or creative dance clearly give the dyspraxic child a better opportunity to work at his own level.

- When choosing teams in PE lessons it is clear that most dyspraxic children rarely have the opportunity to be leaders or captains. To circumvent this problem, teams can be chosen unconventionally. For example, the teacher says, 'Everyone take a ball out of the basket', where there are, say, 12 yellow balls, 12 red balls, 1 blue and 1 green. The teams are formed by the teacher saying, 'Everyone with a yellow ball go to the window end and everyone with a red ball go to the other end. The two people with blue and green balls come to me.' The latter two children are the captains or leaders for the next game. Obviously this particular method can only be used once, but there are many, many ways a creative teacher can sort the class into two teams without the children initially realizing it.

- Use rhythmic speech where possible, with physical tasks. For example, all the children are standing in a circle and throwing and catching a beanbag around the circle. The teacher says 'To Robert' as she throws; Robert looks and chooses and says 'To Sally', and so on. In this way a rhythm can be established. The children are allowed to throw to their immediate neighbours if the circle is large. The use of rhythm in movement has long been thought to be beneficial to children with movement difficulties. 'Rhythmic intention' is a principle of the system of conductive education developed at the Peto Institute in Budapest for children with cerebral palsy.

A useful small booklet entitled *Special Needs Activities* describes activities for PE suitable for a wide range of children with movement difficulties (Knight 1992; see Appendix 1 for details).

Getting changed

This is another difficult area, as the dyspraxic child is often slow getting changed and may seem totally disorganized. Some useful tips:

- Have some seats or benches in the changing room, because it is easier to get changed sitting down and the dyspraxic child is less likely to fall over.

- Ensure that everyone puts the things they have taken off in a set place – for example, on a chair if they are changing in class, or in a bag or a locker.

- Ensure that everyone follows a school uniform labelling policy.

- Have someone check the changing area for missing items after each session. This may save a lot of time hunting for things later on.

- With younger children discuss the organization of clothing as a lesson in itself. For example, 'Put your clothes on your chair. Fold everything neatly. Put each item on the chair in the order you take it off. Put your shoes under the chair. Put your socks in your shoes.'

Art and craft

A lot of organizational skills are needed in art and craft. For example, if a child is painting he will possibly have paints either in pots or on a palette, and water for rinsing his brush along with his brush and paper. There may well be other children sitting round the same table and sharing equipment.

- Use non-spill water and paint pots.

- Ensure surfaces are protected by newspapers.

- Use painting overalls (these can be old shirts).

- Use non-slip mats – they are washable.

- If cutting out is a big problem for the dyspraxic child, the occupational therapist may recommend the use of special spring-loaded scissors (see Appendix 1 for details).

Music

It may well be difficult for the dyspraxic child to beat time, keep rhythm or play softly but the type of activities frequently practised during music lessons can be of enormous benefit in developing rhythm, listening and coordination skills. Again, many other children may well benefit from these activities, which might be suitable for a school lunchtime club. Some examples are listed below.

CLAPPING OR TAPPING SIMPLE RHYTHMS

These can be familiar rhythms such as those produced by tapping out the children's names, addresses, favourite bands or football teams. It can be done by clapping or tapping an instrument such as a wood block or a drum. When the children are familiar with the exercise they can tap their feet to the rhythm as an alternative. They all sit in a circle. To establish a rhythm, the first child taps her rhythm twice: for example, 'Jen-ny Smith, Jen-ny Smith'. Then the whole class joins in – 'Jen-ny Smith, Jen-ny Smith' – then the next child taps his rhythm, and so on.

RECOGNIZING NAME RHYTHMS

The teacher claps a name rhythm, and if a child recognizes her name in the rhythm she stands up (more than one child may have the same rhythm). The teacher carries on with the different rhythms until they are all standing up.

ACTION SONGS

These are good as warming-up or finishing-off exercises. There are lots of action songs that can be used with older children that are not babyish. Examples include 'Underneath the Spreading Chestnut Tree', 'The Hokey-Cokey' and 'Heads, Shoulders, Knees and Toes'. Some suitable books of songs are given in Appendix 1. When doing action songs try to get 'quality' movement. For example, if a movement involves a stretch make sure it's a big one; or if they have to jump, talk about jumping correctly – 'Feet together, knees bend.' These bits can be practised before everyone sings the song. In the Hokey-Cokey, for example, the children have to distinguish between left and right; think which body part they are using; jump in and out with feet together; and do a stretch and a knee bend.

STARTING AND STOPPING

Using an instrument such as a drum, start a simple rhythm such as 'Walk, walk, walk, walk, Wait, wait, wait, wait', and repeat this several times. This activity can also be performed with the children doing four runs (or other types of movement) and four waits, with repeats. In a similar activity, the children move when the drum starts and stop when it stops. Encourage them to listen carefully and to be aware of having to balance when the beat stops. Alternatively, every time the music stops the children move back to their 'spots', as described in the section on PE.

'JOIN IN THE GAME'

This simple song can be found in *Okki-tocki-unga* (see Appendix 1). Add a variety of actions – for example, 'Let everyone jump with me – jump, jump.' Everyone has to do the movement at the correct time in the song and to the correct rhythm. If the action is difficult such as skipping or hopping, then holding hands and doing the movement in a circle helps. When the children are familiar with this song then they can take turns to choose the action.

PLAYING LOUD AND SOFT

The children play on musical instruments to a tune played on the piano or keyboard. Allow them to play as loud as they like as long as they go quiet when you tell them to. Play alternately loud and then soft, and repeat.

PLAYING AND SINGING FAST AND SLOW

Learn a song at normal speed, and when the children know it really well get them to sing it or play along with an instrument really slowly, and then gradually speed up to very fast. This causes great hilarity but the children develop a real understanding of the effect of speed.

PRODUCING VOCAL SOUNDS

The children produce vocal sounds (e.g. ah, oo, ee, ae, mm) to a known tune, and change sound when directed by the teacher. The sound will change several times during the piece, so the children need to listen carefully.

RECOGNIZING INSTRUMENTS FROM THE SOUND

The children have to recognize instruments they know well by their sound (e.g. drum, triangle, wood block, hand bells). The teacher hides behind a screen to play an instrument so that the children cannot see her. One of the children is then asked to either name the instrument or point to his choice from an array of instruments on the table.

Chapter 7

INTERVENTIONS IN SCHOOL

Secondary, Middle or High School and Further Education

WHEN THE CHILD REACHES SECONDARY OR MIDDLE SCHOOL

As noted in Chapter 3, when the dyspraxic child reaches secondary-school age (11 years old) he faces a lot of new challenges. For a start, he is in a much bigger school building. At the beginning of the day he has to go to registration, and he has to change rooms at the end of many of the lessons, carrying most of his books and equipment with him. There are lots of new faces, both adults and children, whereas at his last school he probably knew everybody. He also has to follow a written timetable. There may be new rules such as keeping to the left or right of the corridor when moving around the school. In the canteen or dining room he may have to queue for his lunch, carry a tray and pay for what he has selected. He may well have to catch a bus to school and then find the right bus at the end of the day. At some schools there are large numbers of buses parked outside when it's time to go home.

THE TRANSFER/TRANSITION

It is very important that transfer or transition from the smaller primary school to the much larger secondary school is done sensitively. In the US this refers to the transition from elementary school to middle school or junior high school. The primary SENCO will liaise with his or her secondary colleague about all the children who have special educational needs and discuss what special arrangements may have to be made. There will be opportunities for children to visit their prospective school during the summer term before starting in September. It is important that all teachers, not just the form teacher or SENCO, know what the individual children's difficulties are. Sometimes problems may have to be explained to other staff who come into contact with the children, such as the caretaker, the office and canteen staff.

TRANSITION TO SECONDARY SCHOOL
MARK: A CASE STUDY

Mark's story is most definitely a success story due to good communication between home and school and the positive attitudes on all sides – especially from Mark himself. At the time of writing Mark (aged 11) had been in his first year at secondary school, Year 7, for nearly two months.

Deciding which school

Mark's parents initially considered the possibility of him going to a private school. They went to visit both the private school and his present local authority school. The classes were smaller in the private school and there were computers in every room. 'The only problem was there was a risk of losing his funding which goes with his statement. It wouldn't transfer automatically: you'd have to fight for it.'

They eventually decided for Mark to attend his current school because he would get more individual support from the additional funding and the school has a very good vocational education programme. His mother said, 'I think I've definitely done the right thing because he's got that help and he's a lot more settled. He wouldn't have someone in the class with him like he's got at his present school.' They were also concerned that the private school would be too academic for Mark.

Getting around

The main difference for Mark was the size of the school. He had moved from a small three class primary school to a much larger secondary school of nearly 900 pupils. Finding his way around his new school was the first challenge which began when he made a number of visits to his new school in the term before he started. He was initially worried about getting lost and in fact he did get lost on one of the induction days. He started talking to his friends from his old school during a break time and couldn't find his way back to his class. Sensibly he used his initiative, asked somebody and found his way back to the right classroom. During the induction days Mark was introduced to his tutor group and soon made friends despite there being no one from his old school in his tutor group. He had been given a choice of which tutor group to go into – with the girls from his primary school class, with the boys or to make 'a fresh start'. Mark described making a fresh start as 'going to a different tutor group, knowing nobody and making new friends'.

He had chosen to do this because most of his friends in his class at his primary school were in Year 5 and not transferring to secondary school at the same time as he was. His primary school class had both Year 5 and Year 6 pupils (aged 9–11). He found it hard to leave his Year 5 friends behind. He is gradually making friends in his new class now and has a couple of 'good mates'. Mark agreed that it had been a brave thing to do and said, 'It will help me when I'm older because if I conquer my fear the first time, if I have to do it again it will be pretty easy.'

The children from his primary school had been to the new school twice during the summer term for induction visits. Extra visits were arranged for Mark with his teaching assistant with the specific task of getting used to the geography of his new school. He also went to a parents' evening with his mother and she made sure that he could show her where the classroom for his tutor group was. Initially they had thought about taking photographs of buildings for Mark to look at during the summer before he started but this never happened.

When he started in September he had a lesson timetable and a map of the school. Unfortunately the map was not particularly helpful because it was a poor photocopy and Mark finds maps difficult to read anyway. Mark's tactic was to follow his classmates.

Mark's advice to any new pupils to the school is:

> Check your timetable and the order of your classes. Don't worry for the first couple of weeks because you get longer lunchtimes and more time to get to your classes. It doesn't really matter if you're lost because there's normally the caretaker wandering around or *Sir* [a teacher] or somebody.

Early days – being prepared

Mark's mother thought that he had been well prepared for secondary school but said, 'It's me that wasn't. I think I was worried about him. I probably nagged him quite a bit.' Mark agreed, 'You said "put your tie straight" every morning, "do your top button up" – and nobody does their top button up!'

His mother said that she reminded him to take his mobile phone but to make sure it was switched to silent. He had his phone with him in case there were problems in being picked up by car after school. She also made sure he had his smart card for paying for his school meals and that it was always topped up. Mark had to take a cheque into school to top his smart card up and take it to a certain office to get his card credited. She also gave him four one pound pieces in case he forgot his smart card or did not have enough credit on it. His mother said, 'I think it's such a lot of responsibility, but he's just taken it in his stride.'

Losing PE kit and clothes

Taking care of his PE kit has proved a bit of a problem. The school has a locker system but the lockers are based in their tutorial room and they have free access to this only at the beginning of the day. If they want to get things out of their lockers at lunchtime they have to find a member of staff to unlock the room for them. This meant that on one occasion Mark left his PE kit on a chair in a classroom when he went to lunch and on his return found it had gone missing. With the help of his PE teacher it eventually turned up again about four weeks later. Finding things in Lost Property on his own proved tricky for Mark initially and his PE shirt has also gone missing. There are also penalties for not having the correct PE kit and if this happens three times in a half term, the pupil has to go to detention (i.e. stay behind after school and do some extra work). His mother has to email or send a note to his PE teacher each day he has PE to explain that his kit is missing and that he has got alternative spare clothes in order that he does not get detention. Recently Mark has come home with someone's jumper and has had to take it back and find his own.

Mark has developed strategies for getting changed for PE on time. He says he is now the first of his friends to get changed. His mother said, 'I don't think he undoes the buttons on his shirt and he tends to come home with his shirt inside out. But you don't notice because he's got his blazer on top. It all looks normal and then when he takes it off you can see all the seams.' His mother has always made sure that he wears shoes with Velcro fastenings and although he has been taught to tie his laces, they were always too loose or kept coming undone. One surprising achievement is that he has learned to fasten his tie independently. He kept practising and learned how to do it quite quickly. Mark said that one boy in his class had a problem with putting his tie on and another boy made fun of him. Clearly this has been an important achievement for Mark in gaining peer respect. His mother did investigate if it was possible to get school ties fastened by elastic, Velcro or on a clip but they were not available as part of the school uniform.

A tricky problem

I learned that Mark has had to find out about two unofficial school practices called 'peanutting' and 'pickpocketing'. 'Peanutting' is when the tie is yanked into a small knot like a peanut and 'pickpocketing' when the shirt breast pocket is torn off. Mark has experienced both of these practices at the hands of Year 11 pupils (aged 15–16) who he had been 'messing around with'. He seems fairly unperturbed by the experience, which he described as 'a joke', but his mother notified the school and the practice has now been banned. His mother says that the school quickly deals with these types of issues.

Support in classes

Mark's mother was concerned about individual reading. At primary school Mark had individual reading practice every day and she was concerned that this might not continue at secondary school. However, Mark and some of the other pupils who need extra support are given extra reading during tutorial time on three days a week. Mark is not concerned about missing tutorial time.

Mark's mother said that he has someone in the class to support him during most lessons although the support is for all the pupils who need help and is given in a general way. Overall though his mother considers that he probably has support for more lessons now than he had at primary school. When he was at primary school the support was on an individual basis for half of the time. She said that if there is no one there to help then Mark is totally lost. He needs help generally with reading and writing. Mark finds handwriting takes him a long time and he needs to write slowly in order to keep his writing legible. He can spell short regular words but finds it difficult to spell longer words and he has to think hard to remember them.

At secondary school Mark still has 0.5 support overall and his parents have asked the school to send details of which lessons he has help. 'Now it is different – there is help in most classes but not on a one-to-one basis. During the classes when he needs help there's someone there for him. He's not struggling and that's the main thing.'

Homework and the homework diary

Mark finds it difficult to keep up with his homework diary without support and sometimes he can't work out what he has written when he gets home. His mother said:

> I know he can express himself verbally but he can't write it down accurately and quickly enough on the paper, someone has to do it for him. The first thing Mark did was to write things down in August rather than September because his school diary started in August. They don't give you much space to write in. Quite often they just hand out a homework sheet to complete which is easy so you know what he has to do right away.

Mark's mother sometimes types his homework up for him. She said, 'Obviously if he's got trouble writing down I don't agree with him sitting there for hours handwriting something out. If he tells me, I can type it up for him.'

Special equipment

They have discussed getting Mark a laptop computer to use in school but they do not think he is ready for it yet. Mark uses the computer at home but says that he is not very good at typing. His mother said that he practised his typing skills regularly at primary school and at home on the advice of the Vranch House therapist who recommended a program on the BBC website called Dance Mat typing. (See Appendix 1 for information about Dance Mat typing.) His therapist has told him that this preparation is for the future as she wants him to concentrate on his handwriting at the moment. His mother said that she has noticed a lot of improvement in Mark's handwriting over time. She thinks that in the future he is not going to be able to write quickly enough to get everything written down and will need to use a laptop. She said, 'As he gets older, in a few years time, he'll definitely need one. Then there's the responsibility of looking after it. He's got to carry it round school and to get it home in one piece.' The provision of the laptop is already mentioned in Mark's statement of special educational needs so they are confident that he will get one when he is ready.

Drinking water

Mark likes to drink water which is very good for his health and learning. His mother said, 'He had fun and games the first week because he couldn't work out how to get a drink.'

Initially he took a water bottle to school but still came home very thirsty. He has now found out how to refill his water bottle and has discovered that there are water fountains at school where he can get a drink of water. His mother said, 'He's quite stressed if he can't get a drink of water and he's thirsty.' Unfortunately one solution Mark discovered was buying milk shakes from the school cafeteria, which he would not normally be allowed as he is sensitive to food colourings.

Sporting and leisure activities

Mark has been learning Taekwon-Do for some time and is about to take his black belt as a junior. He has also done a lot of swimming and has a trampoline in the back garden. The trampoline is inset into the ground for safety and he enjoys using it. Mark also recently won second prize in a local competition for his carved pumpkin (Photo 1).

Photo 1

The future

Even though Mark is only 11 years old, he has had some thoughts about what he would like to do when he leaves school. He has decided that he would like to train as a car mechanic or a chef and both of these vocational options are available at his school.

SCHOOL BAGS

One of the biggest problems that the dyspraxic child faces when starting secondary or middle school is the organization and carrying around of his school bag. Often there may be not be any lockers, and the children have to carry extremely heavy bags around with them from lesson to lesson. There has been widespread concern about the health of children's and young people's backs, and parents have been encouraged to buy orthopaedically designed rucksacks, to be worn on both shoulders across the back. Unfortunately, the pupils rarely do this, and in the quick scramble from one lesson to the next they hook their bags over one shoulder. The young dyspraxic person is even less likely to be able to manage to put on a rucksack correctly. Added to this is the problem of organizing the bag and bringing the correct items to school each day. Even when lockers are provided it is difficult for the dyspraxic child to manage their books and equipment for each lesson. They have to return to their locker at break times and remember what they need for their lessons. This may involve repacking their bags which may be time-consuming.

FOLLOWING THE TIMETABLE AND KEEPING TIME

A written timetable can be very difficult for the dyspraxic child to follow. Colour-coding on the timetable can be helpful. The dyspraxic child may find it difficult to orientate himself around this large new building. He may well find that he is the last to leave the class, having spent longer packing his bag, and he does not know where to go to next as everyone else has disappeared.

Having a base to return to, in case of getting lost or experiencing general panic, is advisable for the new child. This may be the SENCO's room or the secretary's office where he can return and be pointed in the right direction.

THE BUDDY SYSTEM

Some schools use a 'buddy system' to help new children who may have difficulty in finding their way around their new school. An older child is asked to help that child initially and to generally 'look out' for him. A development in the United States entitled 'Circle of Friends' has proved very helpful in some schools for all pupils with special needs and it has also been developed in many UK secondary schools. The school sets up a group of friends to support the individual pupil socially – this situation is monitored by trained staff to ensure success for all the pupils involved in the group or circle of friends. Circle of Friends was initially created in 1999 at Santa Monica

High School in California to meet the needs of a socially isolated pupil with special needs. The mission of Circle of Friends is 'to establish an environment of inclusion for teens and young adults with developmental disabilities on middle, high school, and college campuses as well as within their community, focusing on the understanding and acceptance of differences'. More information can be found at www.circleofriends.org (see Appendix 2).

PHYSICAL EDUCATION

There are some particular problems regarding PE at secondary level. At this point team games become much more competitive, and any youngster who seems to be letting the side down by dropping the ball, not catching the ball or missing the ball is made aware by the other children that his performance is not good enough and that he is not a welcome member of the team. If non-competitive options are available, they should be used; it is not sufficient to let the pupil go to the library to catch up on his homework. Many schools now have multigyms available which allow young people to work on their own skills at their own level. As mentioned previously, fitness is often a problem because as dyspraxic children get older they may opt out of physical activity. The young dyspraxic person needs physical education even more than those who have no movement difficulties. Personal fitness programmes and activities such as swimming and trampolining can be based on an individual meeting personal targets – this will not only improve fitness and coordination but also raise self-esteem.

PRACTICAL LESSONS

Lessons such as science and technology often involve using more sophisticated equipment than the young person will have used at primary or elementary school or at home. For example, using cookers, Bunsen burners, woodworking and metalworking equipment or sewing machines can be difficult and even dangerous for the dyspraxic pupil. He may even find unusual seating difficult, such as high laboratory stools. It is important that the individual subject teachers know the problems he is likely to have with equipment. These are lessons in which close supervision is essential and where the learning support assistant can be of invaluable help.

RECORDING WORK

For the young dyspraxic person, recording work may still be a major problem. His handwriting may be more legible but is still likely to be slow and laboured. Taking down homework notes at the end of lessons is going to be difficult if these are quickly dictated or have to be copied from the blackboard. Digital recorders or even mobile phones (if permitted) can be used for taking notes. Word-processing for homework should be considered as an option. If necessary, the use of a portable laptop computer should be allowed. Even this has its difficulties because the laptop is yet another heavy item to add to the school bag – and an expensive one if it is mislaid. Palm top or notebook computers may seem a good option but unfortunately the keyboards are often very small and difficult to use for pupils with fine motor difficulties. The pupil also needs to know where he can print work out from his laptop.

Photocopied notes prepared by the teacher are invaluable. Alternatively, a learning support assistant could make notes and photocopy them at the end of a lesson for any child in the class with special needs.

Reading maps, diagrams and music

These activities may well be difficult for the dyspraxic child as they involve interpreting abstract symbols and/or obtaining detail from a complex visual presentation. The use of simplified maps and diagrams will help – colour-coding is helpful here. Colour-coding can also be used when simple written music is being introduced.

Examinations

Consider in advance whether the dyspraxic child needs extra time or an amanuensis (a person such as a learning support assistant or teacher acting as a scribe) for examinations. For external exams these concessions have to be applied for well in advance and may require the support of a statement of special educational needs or other reports from the school or from other professionals.

Build up his confidence!

The child will become more independent as his confidence is built up. Success in itself builds confidence. Praise for good work and good effort should not be neglected, even if the targets achieved are small ones.

ANDY: A CASE STUDY
Secondary school

At primary school Andy did not remember finding things difficult at all. He went to a relatively small primary school with one class per year group. They had some teaching assistant support and he remembers that one boy had individual support within the class.

When he was in his first year at secondary school the special needs department suggested he went to Vranch House for assessment and advice. His main problems at school were handwriting and catching the ball in PE. Andy recalled, 'I used to be about 12 foot away from it – so if the ball landed *there*, I'd be over *here* trying to catch it.'

He remembered his assessment consisting of the therapist going through fine and gross motor skills including handwriting tasks. Following the assessment she sent Andy and his parents a copy of the report that she also sent to the special needs coordinator (SENCO) at his school with advice on what support Andy needed. Andy said that due to this 'By the time I left the SEN department I was probably one of the least troublesome students they had.' In the time Andy was at the school he recalled that the SEN department got funding for more equipment and extra staff to support pupils. When he left there was a teaching/learning support assistant in each of the lowest level sets from Year 7 to Year 11.

When he was taking his examinations he was allowed to use a word processor with the spell check and grammar check turned off for the English exam. He got extra time for all his exams but found this most helpful when taking the English exam.

Andy said that his coordination improved in the time he was at secondary school and he was aware that there were other pupils who had greater difficulties than he had.

Andy had learning support assistant help only for English. This support was not one-to-one but for the whole class. Andy felt that staying in the lower set for English actually had a detrimental effect on his GCSE (General Certificate of Secondary Education) results and thought that he should have been moved up to the next ability set in English following his Key Stage 3 assessment in Year 9.[1]

> After I'd done my Key Stage 3 SATs I was hoping that I'd move up to Set 4. Set 5 was the lowest set and therefore nobody wanted to teach it and Set 1 was for all the academics doing English literature as well as English language. The first time round I got a 'D' but I think that was partly due to the fact that the teacher, who was OK, spent most of his time trying to deal with troublesome students. There was a core of between five to ten difficult students and we were in a very large set

---

1 At the time Andy was at school all UK pupils were assessed during Year 9 (Key Stage 3 standard assessment tests (SATs)). This was discontinued from 2009.

of about thirty-five. I was just frustrated that I was in that set because I didn't do too badly, I got a 4 or 5 in my SATs which isn't brilliant but still it's not bad. I thought from the rumours I heard that I was going to be moved up a set and I was hoping for that but unfortunately I was still in the set that I had been in from Year 9 – the bottom set – it was really annoying.

Andy felt that he had been held back because of this and achieved only a grade D. He took the English exam again when he was in the Lower Sixth Form (aged 16–17). He said that this time:

I had a decent teacher and was in a much smaller group. I didn't have help from the SENCO but I just cracked on with it and because we were in the lower sixth all of us wanted to get the GCSE. I didn't go on to the higher paper I just took the foundation paper but I got a 'C' straight off of that so it makes you wonder what would have happened if I'd taken the higher paper.[2]

Andy mainly had problems with handwriting. 'I've always read quite a lot, so my spellings are OK but as with most people there's odd words that you can't spell. You have your odd blank moment where you just can't spell anything.'

With regard to sport, Andy found that his coordination difficulties made a difference in rounders during the summer, but not when he was playing football and rugby. He said:

Generally if the rugby ball came my way, it was aimed at me and it's big enough to be able to catch even with very bad hand eye coordination. I did get selected for the rugby team for some odd reason and did a few slalom races as well with the canoe club.

Andy had joined his local canoeing club when he was in Year 6 following a three-day adventure course organized when he was at primary school. One of the former club leaders ran the course in a number of primary schools in the area. The course consisted of activities such as canoeing, pony trekking and trekking along the coastal paths. Andy was particularly interested in canoeing following this course. His parents took him to attend training sessions at the local club and Andy is now himself a coach.

Andy said that the ethos at his secondary school was very good and there was no bullying:

---

2   A grade C was the maximum Andy could achieve on this particular paper. If he had taken the alternative papers he might have achieved a grade A or B.

It wasn't really that sort of school. The school was very tough on that and even at the slightest sign of bullying you were automatically warned and if you took it any further you were internally suspended. There was no form of bullying at all throughout, when I've talked to other people from other schools there's been reports of heavy drug use and all that sort of stuff. My school is one of the most popular schools in the area and when I left they had 150 places with 300 kids vying for those places.

When Andy went there it was one of two local schools he could have attended and he had no difficulties getting in. Now it is more difficult because there have been more people moving into the area and other people wanting to attend the school from further afield because of its reputation.

Andy's advice to a pupil who has just moved to secondary school and might be experiencing difficulties is:

Go and talk to the people in the SEN department because they're paid to deal with it. The other teachers are already harassed enough but you can talk to people more easily in there. They're not *just* teachers they're people and it's not just a job to them, they enjoy doing it.

Further education college

After doing a year in the Lower Sixth Form at his secondary school Andy decided to go to his local further education college to complete his Advanced Level exams. When Andy went to college his class had a learning support assistant for all the lessons during the first year. In the second year, however, they had an assistant for only one two-hour lesson a week. This was because there was not sufficient funding from the local authority for more time. He said in retrospect:

If I had been more conscious of things and how local government works back then I would have sent a message to the principal of the college and to somebody in County Hall asking why there wasn't enough funding. It's all very well having somebody supporting the first years but you're kind of letting the side down if there isn't that support for second years. You're defeating the purpose because you helped people pass the first year and now they're not going to have that much help for the second year.

The classes consisted of about 30 students. The learning support assistant helped generally in the class with students who needed help. Andy suggests that if a student needs more individual help the best strategy is: 'Keep that person in all the lessons but also arrange a mutual time to meet up [i.e. with the Learning Support Assistant], have a quiet area and just go through the work and see if there are any problems.'

Chapter 8

HOW CAN PARENTS
HELP THEIR CHILD?

EARLY DAYS

Many parents develop a number of strategies through necessity and experience. Some good ideas suggested to me by parents of dyspraxic children are included in this chapter. There are many activities that can be carried out at home before the child goes to school.

Trust your instincts

The persons who know a child best are his parents. Many may be uneasy about their child's development, particularly if the dyspraxic child is not their first, but may be told by health professionals and general practitioners that he is just a slow developer and a little delayed in his milestones.

Sophie's mother said:

> She had her three-and-a-half-year check and I said to the doctor that I was really worried that she couldn't ride a bike. She was just pushing along with her feet. He said, 'Oh I'm not worried about that.' You couldn't put your finger on what it was. We hadn't heard of dyspraxia or any sort of developmental delays or anything. My husband was really worried that she couldn't draw a person – other people at his work had two-year-olds who were drawing pictures of people. Everyone kept saying, 'Oh, she's fine.'

Emma's mother recalled that the health visitor had said, 'Oh, she's all right, she's a late developer.' Emma's mother said:

When she was going to start school I said to the teacher, 'I don't think things are right. I can't teach her to write her name. She doesn't know how to spell', and she said 'Oh, she's a late developer', and we had this for ages from the school. I kept being told, 'There's no problem', and I kept saying, 'Yes there is.' You don't know who to get hold of, nobody seems to know anything about it.

I took her to see the doctor because she kept falling over and asked if there was something wrong with her. He sent us to the orthopaedic hospital and they decided there wasn't anything wrong with her legs or her feet but they thought it might have been her eyesight because she has got a squint. She wasn't holding a pencil or anything in the right fashion and she used to scribble, and she wasn't making the same progress as Claire [older daughter] had made at the same age.

Paul's mother said of the speech and language therapist:

I began to feel I was perhaps being seen as a sort of over-anxious, pushy parent. I was saying there must be some reason for his speech delay. I really thought she had got me down as somebody who expects their children to be reading. This was when he was three and a half and he was still in nappies. She sort of sat down with a sigh and said, 'Children develop differently'. I know that, I do know that, but I felt that there was some reason for Paul having this speech problem.

It is important for parents to realize that their child's progress is likely to be seen as delayed development, and the other problems displayed by dyspraxic children that the parents are aware of are not likely to be apparent in a clinical situation or on a home visit. With young children the difference between a small developmental delay and a more significant one is not very great. It is only as the child gets older and starts primary or elementary school that the differences become more apparent to those outside the home. So if a parent believes that there is a problem, he or she must not give up, but be persistent.

Many parents report early problems with feeding. Sophie had problems very early:

When she was a month old she had to go into hospital because she was down to five pounds. Basically I didn't have enough milk. I think what had happened is that she was very fussy about latching on. The midwife kept coming round and watching me feed and said everything was fine. They left it too long, it was nearly four weeks. She seemed so content – she was really sleepy, she didn't cry and we didn't know she was hungry. We thought everything was fine. So then she started having bottles and she gained weight quite steadily. But when she was a year old that was when I really started to worry because she just seemed so undeveloped compared to all the other children. I remember taking her to her first birthday party and they were all moving around the room and eating biscuits. Sophie couldn't chew anything.

As described in Chapter 3, Paul's problem was the opposite in that he would eat too much:

He would prefer to eat with his hands, but since he's been at school we've been working on that. We've been working on eating and swallowing and slowing down and keeping his mouth closed when he eats and he's not so messy now. He is not to rush off and do something else until the meal is over. He still chokes a bit but not as much.

Problems often continue as the child goes through school. Emma, aged nearly ten, still finds mealtimes difficult. Her father reported:

You see, usually in the morning after breakfast I wash up and usually Andrew [younger brother] wipes up. To get Emma to come out and wipe up was quite a job. I think she finds it difficult but recently she's come out and she's given a hand. She lays the table, not much trouble about that. She uses a knife and a fork but she drops no end of food, she's a messy eater.

Her mother said:

She still can't cut up. She can't hold and use her knife for cutting up. If she's not looking what she's doing she can quite easily tip the cup or glass. I daren't fill them very full – near the top and they'd be over.

Her father said that she wants to do things even though they are difficult for her, and will want to carry the drinks from the kitchen to the living room: 'I'll say about being careful with it and she'll usually get it to her mother without spilling it. She's a good trier.'

Getting the child to do these things is not always easy and there may be many spillages on the way, but clearly these are things that children can do as they mature, and they will be proud of being able to do household chores like their brothers and sisters. There are many ways of helping a child to develop these skills:

- Use non-slip mats under plates and cups.

- Use larger-handled cutlery. An alternative is to put foam grips on normal cutlery.

- Don't fill cups and beakers to the top.

- Use plates and bowls with lips so that the food is less likely to end up on the table. Special plates, cups and cutlery can be obtained – if your child has an occupational therapist, she is the best person to ask. In the UK Nottingham Rehab produce a catalogue of items that can be purchased. In the US a useful source of equipment is the OT Practice Buyers Guide (see 'special equipment' in Appendix 1 for details).

- Ensure the child is seated properly at the table, ideally with feet flat and elbows at table height and with enough room on either side of him so that he does not interfere unknowingly with other family members.

- Whereas small children may wear a bib, this is not appropriate for older children, but they can use napkins tucked under their chin.

- Make sure all contents of packed lunches are easy to unwrap and easy to handle. With pre-packed yogurts it is difficult to remove the tops without the contents splashing over the person opening them. Carbonated drinks are likely to 'explode'. Crisp packets are often difficult to undo without the contents flying out. So put all drinks and foods into easy-opening containers. Put in easy-to-peel fruit such as bananas.

- Unsliced bread is a useful snack for children with chewing problems. This cannot be eaten quickly and forces the child to chew and exercise his jaw, lips and tongue muscles.

Sleeping

Some parents report that their children were unusually sleepy and contented babies, whereas others report difficulties with their babies settling and being erratic sleepers.

Paul's mother said:

> Paul never slept well, he was always hard to settle and we didn't have an unbroken night until he was three and a half. He always napped well during the day but he used to tear around and then he'd just flake out. When he was a baby that was for three or four hours. You see, I always had this ideal picture of Paul as an easy baby because he was just so happy all the time. So, yes, he did have sleeping difficulties but if he had been an unhappy child that would have been more of a problem.

Now at nearly eight years of age, 'his sleeping is much better than it's ever been, but it's not unknown for Paul to wake at half past four or come to our bed at half past five'.

If your child wakes during the night, then keep him as active as possible during the day and discourage naps. When he does wake reassure him, and then if he will not settle, encourage him to do something quiet such as looking at a book, listening to a music tape or to a story through headphones. Have a nightlight in the room so that he does not feel frightened if he wakes. As he reaches school age he is not very likely to have the opportunity to nap during the day, so often the sleeping problems disappear.

Talking

Speech is often delayed with children with dyspraxia, although parents usually are not initially worried because the child usually has a good understanding of language. Sophie's mother reported:

> She seemed really bright, she seemed to understand everything but she didn't talk. She didn't start talking until she was way past three. At the nursery she went to, when she was nearly three and a half, they said I ought to think about seeing a speech and language therapist, and then that Easter she just started talking. She just came out with all these nursery rhymes and songs. They all came out from nowhere. I mean, she'd had odd words, and if she wanted something like a biscuit she'd just point at it and whine and whine. We'd spend half an hour getting her to say 'biscuit' and she just wouldn't. Looking back on it you'd say it's really stupid that I didn't realize, but I suppose it was because she was the first child. Sophie just seemed to understand. If you asked her to point to any part of her body she could do it and she could follow instructions.

Emma also started talking late, but her parents put it down initially to the fact that her sister, Claire, who was nearly two years older, used to talk for her. 'If you asked Emma a question Claire would always answer for her. We had this problem for ages. We kept saying "Let her answer for herself".'

Paul's speech was also delayed; by the age of three and a half he was still only speaking a few words and they were not clear. His mother recalled:

> I thought it was odd, his speech delay, because he was obviously a bright child and his social skills were good. He interacted well right from a very early age with smiling and pointing and eye contact. They were all extremely good so I thought this speech delay was odd as he was developing well in other areas.

There are many activities that parents can carry out at home that will help to encourage language development. They are no different from those that any parent would carry out with non-dyspraxic children, but it is important not to abandon them because your child does not give a verbal response or loses interest in a short time. Try these:

- Reading stories and looking at picture books.

- Saying and singing nursery rhymes.

- Playing games like 'pat-a-cake', 'round and round the garden' and 'peek-a-boo'.

- Short and sweet and often is better than sessions that last a long time and become a battle to keep your child's attention. Stop as soon as he loses concentration.

Crawling and walking

Children with dyspraxia often walk late and may not crawl or may have unusual crawling patterns. Lisa did not walk until she was 19 months, and her mother said she realized that although this was not unusually late, 'She didn't seem to be very strong with it. She was very late pushing up on her hands, on her front palms and that sort of thing.'

Sophie walked at the same age but did not crawl. Her mother recalled that at a birthday party with other children:

she used to sit on the spot and she couldn't reach the toys and then she'd just give up. My friend had a baby-bouncer and we put her in and she just pulled her legs up, she wouldn't touch the floor. She never pulled herself up to walk round the furniture. She never crawled, and then she started bottom-shuffling and she would even bottom-shuffle through a tunnel and she'd go really, really quickly. She would do a lot of hand-flapping. One day when she was 19 months she very, very shakily stood up and stumbled across the room and then she started walking.

In contrast, Emma walked early, at ten months. 'She didn't crawl very much but when she did she always went backwards and not forwards.'

There are a number of resources that can be used to help pre-school children improve their motor skills. 'Tumble Tots', 'Gymbabes' and 'Gymbobs' is a national UK network of gym clubs for young children aged six months to seven years. A similar club in the US is My Gym for children aged from six weeks to 13 years. Most local gymnastic clubs also have sessions for babies and toddlers. The British Gymnastics association has developed the 'FUNdamental Movement Ideas for Early Years' scheme especially for younger children from walking to six years old. Also the Youth Sport Trust has a number of programmes such as 'Active Play' for four to seven year olds and 'Start to Play' for children from birth to five years old. In the US the main organisation is USA Gymnastics. There is also a national program entitled Let's Move, which is designed to help children and young people live healthier and more active lives. See Appendix 2 for further information about these schemes.

Private play areas for toddlers may have soft play areas, ball pools and appropriate toys. The best way to find out what is available locally is to ask your child's occupational therapist or physiotherapist, the staff at playgroup or nursery, the pre-school advisory teacher or other parents. If all else fails try the local library, civic centre or town hall or Yellow Pages.

Sensory awareness

Dyspraxic children can show an oversensitivity to sensory stimulation, whether in response to noise or to tactile stimuli.

NOISE SENSITIVITY

Paul's mother recalled that, although he was a very confident child and not likely to be upset by anything:

> Once getting out of the car at a friend's house, the children in the house were upstairs banging on the window but we couldn't see them. Paul was really scared and he couldn't see what was making the noise. It wasn't particularly loud. It didn't make me jump. He will say now about the radio or music, 'It's giving me a headache.'

Sophie's mother said:

> From a very young age certain toys made her hysterical and upset. She had a little doggie and when it barked she used to really cry and cry. She had a musical doll that my husband's parents had given her and they had to hide it away because she got so distressed. It is smell as well, certain smells she can't stand. I always remember when I sat in on the first group she went to at Vranch, it was really funny – it was quite a relief as well. The children were all sitting in the hall and somebody moved a chair on the other side of a screen, and about five of them turned round and said, 'What was that?' It was in stereo, all five of them at the same time.

As an older child Emma still does not like school discos – she tells her parents, 'It's too noisy and I don't like the lights.'

Lisa was also sensitive to noise when she was a baby. Her mother said:

> She absolutely hated me using the vacuum cleaner until she was about two. At that age we bought her a toy vacuum cleaner and that really helped her to overcome it. We also moved to a slightly bigger house which meant I could put her at one end and start vacuuming the other end. As a small baby things like a lorry going past on the road would make her cry and she still has an incredible sensitivity to alarms. We have a burglar alarm and a smoke alarm and even when you set the alarm you can see her slightly tensing up just because it beeps. She's used to it now, which is good, but one night the smoke alarm malfunctioned – there was no fire or smoke or anything and it wasn't even making the noise it was meant to make. It was just making a high-pitched whistle. For about a week afterwards she couldn't sleep in her own bed, she was so upset by it and so worried about it going off again. She is very, very sensitive to certain noises but not to noise overall.

TACTILE SENSITIVITY

Paul was sensitive to things on his skin. His mother said that as a pre-school child he didn't like water getting on his clothing and making it wet. Emma's parents found that as a baby she reacted when the car started moving:

> You know, when you put a child in the car it usually sends them to sleep. When we put Emma in the car as soon as it started she would bawl, she went on for ages. She was never sick but as soon as the car started moving she'd start crying.

DEPTH PERCEPTION

Paul's mother also recalled how he was not sensitive enough to certain visuomotor stimuli:

> I remember once when he was crawling. He was only about 11 months or so and we were in a friend's garden which was a sort of terraced lawn but with quite a drop. I was watching him and he crawled right up to the edge of this drop. He looked over and studied it and he was about to lower himself off. There was no way he could manage that drop. I thought that was odd because young babies don't do that, they have depth perception.

(See footnote 2 on p.27.)

THE SCHOOLCHILD

First days at school

Starting school may be a difficult time, especially as nowadays reception or kindergarten classes are often more formal than they used to be a few years ago, with more structured literacy and numeracy activities. Often the dyspraxic child has loved nursery or playgroup and enjoyed the freedom of being able to go from one activity to the next without having to sit down, be still and listen for more than a short while.

Paul had loved his playgroup, but within two weeks of starting full time at school things were clearly wrong.

> He was terrible and was having temper tantrums. He had never been a child with this kind of problem. He was saying, 'It's too hard, I can't do it, it's too hard.' The first half-term was difficult as he didn't want to go to school. He was a school refuser, actually. It made me realize how difficult it is if you have a child who is refusing to go, because it's really hard to get them there. He was taking his uniform off as fast as I was getting it on. I had to carry him to get him to school, so it was very traumatic. It was really awful the first few weeks, but I think he had quite a hard time because it was quite a structured first class. The teacher has them in her class for two years and she has them all reading. They spend a lot of time sitting at desks, which Paul hated. He couldn't do all these tasks they were asking him to do, things like getting changed for PE.

The important thing is for parents to talk to the class teacher about any problems their child is experiencing as soon as they become apparent. The parents of a dyspraxic child should make the school aware of any difficulties before the child starts school, so as to alert the teacher to the fact that sitting still for long periods may be difficult and to raise awareness of those difficulties described in Chapter 6.

Dressing

The dyspraxic child is likely to struggle with getting ready for school in the mornings when everyone is busy and time is limited. As noted earlier, getting changed before and after PE or swimming, putting coats on and taking them off at the beginning and end of school and playtimes are also difficult.

SOPHIE, AGED SEVEN

She gets undressed. She's got Velcro shoes. She's a lot better, she can put her socks on now. She's got this thing that she can't do her shoes up tightly enough. She always says, 'It's not tight enough' and that drives us mad. She always has to ask which way round her knickers go and which way round her vest goes. When she comes home she's always really tired and she can't manage to get her sweatshirt off very well. She can do buttons now but she cannot do jeans' buttons and zips. We haven't really attempted laces yet.

LISA, AGED NINE

She still gets in a hopeless muddle if her clothes are inside out. She tends to cast them off, just in a heap, before she goes to bed. I make sure they are all the right way round for the next morning and that the last thing she has to put on is at the bottom of the pile and then she can work down the pile. She takes a terrific amount of organizing. Every day she will come out of school minus something or other that she needs for the evening, and often with her shoes on the wrong feet. That's absolutely classic, really isn't it? Her buckles are half undone and her tights are inside out. She's always a little bit muddled. It does take her longer. She asks for help wherever she can. With doing up shoes she's always very reluctant to spend the time to persevere and do it herself. She'd rather just ask someone else to do it for her. It's always difficult striking a balance. On the one hand you feel it's really good for her to have as much practice as she can, but then she gets so frustrated.

EMMA, AGED TEN

She cannot do things like tying up shoelaces, she has difficulty with buttons and left and right. I leave little markers to show which shoe goes on which foot. Sometimes she has got things on back to front. You tend to buy shoes and clothes that you know she's not going to have too much difficulty getting on and she'll be able to find the right way so that then she is more independent. Sometimes she does not know which way her shoes or clothing go and she has to ask, which she finds frustrating. She used to have problems doing up shoes, you know, buckles as well. She mastered buckles about three years ago. It took her ages to get the thing in the right holes. Gloves or mittens are another thing she has problems with. With gloves she can never work out which finger goes in which hole. You sort of get two or three fingers together. There are some mittens that she can never seem to get the thumb in so she's usually thumbless. She doesn't like mittens very much.

Helping children with dressing

There are lots of ploys that parents use to help their children with dressing – some of the main ones are listed below:

LABEL ALL CLOTHES

All children lose their clothes at school from time to time but the dyspraxic child is likely to do this more often than most, so ensure that all clothes are labelled with your child's name.

LABEL SHOES 'LEFT' AND 'RIGHT'

Shoes can be marked 'left' and 'right'. Some people use the letters L and R and some use colours such as red and green. The origins of using red for left and green for right can be quite interesting for a child and might fire his imagination. The nautical use of green for right (starboard) and red for left (port) in lights for boats, ships and aeroplanes can be seen if you live near the sea or an airport. The old nautical saying, 'The captain left his red port wine behind', might also intrigue your child. You could tell your child to hold his hands in front of him, palms downwards with the thumbs out – in this position the left hand makes the shape of a capital L. You could use a red capital L in left shoes and a green capital R in right shoes. Another useful tip (for right-handed children only) is to say 'I write with my right hand.'

USE VELCRO FASTENING

The Velcro method of fastening can be used on all sorts of clothing. Nowadays shoes for both children and adults commonly have Velcro fastenings. Jackets often incorporate both zips and Velcro. Velcro is easier and quicker than laces and zips and buttons.

DISTINGUISH FRONT FROM BACK

Another difficulty is knowing which is the front and which is the back of a jumper or other item of clothing. Point out to your child that a label is always at the back. In addition, having a distinctive pattern on the front often helps.

MAKE SURE THAT GARMENTS ARE LARGE ENOUGH

All children have experienced times when their head and ears are stuck in the neck of their jumper. Make sure this does not happen by ensuring that your child's clothes are reasonably loose and easy to pull on and off. If they are too big, however, he will find sleeves that are too long a distraction and a nuisance.

USE ELASTIC IN WAISTS AND WITH BUTTONS

Elastic-waisted skirts and trousers make things much easier. Often school uniforms nowadays are much easier to take on and off, with T-shirts, polo shirts, sweatshirts and jogging pants being quite common. Adding loops of elastic to button holes can often help to make fastening easier. Fastening gloves to each other with a long length of elastic threaded through armholes may be practical and helpful with the very young, but is frowned upon by most children of school age as babyish and consequently may cause more problems than it solves. Adaptations to clothing have to be done sensitively, as today's children are often very definite from quite a young age about what they find acceptable to wear.

SORT OUT THE SWIMMING KIT

Getting tight-fitting swimming costumes on and off can be a nightmare, so ensure that costumes and trunks are easy to put on and remove. Having a distinctive towel is useful, so that your child knows at a glance which is his. A swimming bag should be large enough to get the towel in after it has been used and is no longer neatly folded. Include a plastic carrier bag to put the wet costume in as soon as it is taken off so that the dry clothes do not get wet.

CHOOSE A SENSIBLE SCHOOL BAG

School bags should be practical – not too big, but large enough for your child's purpose at the stage of schooling he is at. A distinctive style is helpful, so that he recognizes his bag quickly. Often schools nowadays have uniform school bags, which makes it more difficult. If the school permits, use stickers to make the bag more easily recognizable.

CHECK LOOPS ON COATS

Many young children have difficulty in hanging their coats on hooks because the loop inside the collar is too small for them to be able to manage it. Making a bigger loop will not only ensure that the child achieves this task but also mean that the coat is not lying on the floor all day – possibly getting trampled on by passing feet.

TIES

Some schools still require children to wear neck-ties; in fact there has been a resurgence of ties recently in school uniforms. Tying them is a perennial problem for many schoolchildren. Either use elastic or even better Velcro: point out that the police have this type of fastening for safety!

ORGANIZING

Initially you will be organizing your child's day and remembering things such as the school bag and the packed lunch, and you will be aware of his timetable. Most parents find it helpful to start involving children in this organization as soon as possible – to go through questions such as 'What day is it tomorrow? What lessons do you have tomorrow? Have you got your reading book, homework, swimming things?' Gradually the child will begin to take responsibility for this, but will have benefited from having had a routine built up by his parents. Every evening, encourage him to think about which day it is tomorrow, what he will need and whether he has the routine things he needs every day, such as his packed lunch. Pictorial lists or timetables will help. These can be hand-drawn, or use pictures cut out of magazines.

Try to make this time fun and special for your child. Do not involve brothers and sisters in the exercises, as they will undoubtedly do better. Make it your special time with your child.

Remind him about his homework. Talk to the school if problems seem to be developing. If his homework takes him an inordinate amount of time compared to other children, let the school know.

ENCOURAGING LEISURE ACTIVITIES

It is important for children as they get older to develop leisure activities and hobbies. If a child has a real interest in an activity, he will become enthusiastic and achieve levels that may seem unlikely at first. Fitness is of particular importance because, as mentioned earlier, children who are not very able at physical activities tend to avoid them and become less fit. Generally non-competitive sports should be encouraged, such as swimming, horse riding, trampolining and bicycle riding. All these activities are good for developing coordination and fitness as well as being enjoyable. Some children do develop interests in sports which may be perceived as difficult, but through perseverance they often manage to achieve success. Parents' reports of children with dyspraxia mentioned one individual who had become a member of the school football team and another who enjoyed ballet and tap lessons. The discipline of sports from the East such as tai chi, yoga, judo and Taekwon-Do is very helpful for these children as it helps to develop and improve the core stability of the body. Mark (case study, p.68) is about to take his black belt as a junior at the age of 11 years. (See Appendix 2 to find out more about Taekwon-Do instruction.)

Small-scale apparatus in the garden can help your child develop skills in a protected, non-competitive environment. Swings, slides, climbing frames and trampettes (small trampolines) can all be purchased for home use. Regularly following home exercise programmes set by the physiotherapist can make a big difference. Paul's mother said:

> What we found he really liked and I think is really helpful are all sorts of board games, dominoes and playing cards. We are teaching him to play bridge. He's really interested in it and very motivated and it has a lot of skills. You have to be able to count the points, to remember what's gone and to take turns. So we do a lot of those games.

Many children develop an interest in computer games. Often the standard mouse is difficult for them to control at first, especially using the drag-and-click facility. There are a number of types of children's mouse or roller-balls available, which they often find easier initially.

RELATIONSHIPS WITH OTHER CHILDREN

Often the dyspraxic child has difficulties in developing friendships. He or she may tend to play more with younger children. Lisa's mother reported:

> She has never really had a close friendship that has lasted. She likes younger children who she can mother and she likes older children who will mother her, but it's quite difficult for her to have an equal relationship with a child of her own age.

Often the child develops a close friendship with another child who has similar difficulties, and this may well turn out to be a long-lasting relationship.

Give him credit for effort!

Parents know that their child often works very hard but gets very little credit for it. A dyspraxic child often has to put out an enormous amount of effort to do something that another child can do easily. He will often be very tired at the end of the day.

Praise is a great motivator, and it is important to give credit for effort expended along the way rather than just for the end result.

Chapter 9

THERAPEUTIC INTERVENTIONS

PHYSIOTHERAPY AND OCCUPATIONAL THERAPY
Research

It is difficult to prove whether a long-term programme of therapy has benefited a group of children or not because it is impossible to know what their progress would have been like without the intervention. A number of intervention programmes described here indicate that children do benefit. Williams, Smith and Ainsley (1999) carried out a study with a group of 15 children with developmental coordination problems. The children were assessed using the Movement ABC before and after a ten-week intervention programme and were found to have shown improvement in overall performance, particularly with ball-related skills. The intervention programme consisted of a 45-minute session once a week, supported by a home exercise programme. In the first stage of a long-term study Losse *et al.* (1991) found that when the children designated as 'clumsy' took part in a year-long intervention programme, many of them made significant progress in the area of learning motor skills.

Common sense would lead us to believe that if we find certain skills difficult and we practise them regularly, they are likely to improve. If we do not practise them or even actively avoid doing them they may become worse, and certainly an individual's confidence in carrying out these skills will diminish.

The North Devon Children's Physiotherapy Department carried out a survey to examine the effectiveness of therapeutic intervention with regard to the children with dyspraxia (Sylvester 1999). Questionnaires were sent to referrers, teachers, parents and children in respect of 41 children who had received physio treatment in the preceding 12 months: 94 per cent of respondents said that the report, advice or intervention received had added to their understanding of the dyspraxic child's difficulties. Improvements were seen in the areas of handwriting, self-esteem and PE by over 70 per cent of the respondents.

Individual therapy

Some children may be offered individual therapy sessions over a period of time. The therapist may also give a home exercise programme for parents to practise with their child, and may give advice to his school on how to plan activities for him in PE lessons.

Group therapy

Group sessions may be offered at a specialist centre, or at the child's school if there is a large enough group of children who would benefit from such sessions. Usually groups are small – no more than eight children. Again, the therapist may offer home exercise programmes and advice to the school on PE.

Activities: gross motor skills

Group and individual sessions will focus on a number of areas.

BALL SKILLS
Activities can include catching, throwing, rolling, aiming and kicking, using a variety of balls and beanbags, as appropriate.

BALANCE AND COORDINATION

- Doing activities such as walking, running, hopping, skipping, jumping and cycling.

- Following different tracks or patterns on the floor, walking, running or cycling along a slalom course, using cones.

- Using ropes for skipping and jumping.

- Changing direction during a movement and maintaining balance.

- Maintaining a balance when stopping or when in a held position.

- Balancing in various positions such as on one leg, in a squat position, from all fours, and lifting different combinations of arms and legs.

- Moving forwards, backwards and sideways.

- Rolling sideways and forwards.

SWIMMING, HYDROTHERAPY AND AQUATIC THERAPY

Swimming is particularly helpful for children with coordination difficulties because they have the support of the water when they are moving in the pool. Therapeutic swimming programmes such as the Halliwick method involve the children in the following activities:

- Developing breath control by learning to blow out in the water.

- Learning to walk, jump and move in a controlled manner in the pool.

- Learning to enter the water safely from the side.

- Developing a controlled float and maintaining stillness in the water.

- Becoming safe in the water by developing swimming skills.

The Halliwick method was established in 1949 by James McMillan at the Halliwick School for Girls in London. The children are taught swimming on a one-to-one basis but within a group-based activity. The Halliwick Association of Swimming Therapy arranges courses to train instructors in the methodology and will know where Halliwick swimming is taught in an area (see Appendix 2 for contact details).

TRAMPOLINING AND REBOUND THERAPY

Working individually with the therapist, the dyspraxic child discovers the many benefits of trampolining, or rebound therapy. The general benefits are that the limbs become stronger, and muscle tone improves along with stamina and general coordination. Other specific benefits are improvement in reaction speed, in spatial awareness and in body awareness, and improved height and depth perception.

Activities: fine motor skills

If the physiotherapist and occupational therapist are working as a team, this area is more usually covered by the occupational therapist.

HAND FUNCTION

Hand function activities may include painting and drawing exercises, craft activities and cooking, as well as simple exercises to improve hand function.

DAILY-LIVING SKILLS

The therapist will usually provide help and guidance with mealtime skills, including the use of cutlery; dressing skills; toileting skills; seating and general posture. Normally she will advise parents on improving these skills and on any suitable equipment that might be needed. The therapist may also visit the school and advise on these areas if necessary.

HANDWRITING

The therapist will recommend suitable writing equipment, seating position, posture and pencil control. Activities will include pencil and pen exercises involving tracking from left to right, making up and down strokes, and developing flow by doing a series of writing patterns. She will not usually work on set writing schemes because, if the child is working in a group, all the children may be from different schools, which may have different writing schemes. The skills worked on will be those that will help the child to develop the skills he will need whichever writing scheme he is using.

SPEECH AND LANGUAGE THERAPY

Speech and language therapy may be delivered individually or in a small group. It may be offered at a centre or carried out at the child's school. The speech and language therapist will also offer advice on home programmes. She may give the teaching assistant programmes of work to carry out in school. She may also give advice if the child has difficulties with eating and saliva control.

Activities

- Motor skill training, which involves speech movements and sounds; sometimes movement exercises are done before speech is practised. The Nuffield Centre Dyslexia Programme uses this type of approach (Connery et al. 1992).

- Activities for developing pragmatic communication skills (i.e. social communication).

- Activities for developing receptive and expressive language.

- In some cases signing may be recommended to support developing speech; Makaton signing is often used (Walker 1976).[1]

---

1   Makaton signing is a simplified version of British Sign Language, with a small core vocabulary of about 350 language concepts. Key signs only are signed along with normal grammatical speech. In the US a simplified form of American Sign Language is used. This is reflected in other countries, which also use simplified forms of their own sign language.

VRANCH HOUSE

At Vranch House, the children receive their therapy in groups as well as individual and home programmes. Group work means that more children can be given help and that they have the benefit of working with other children with similar difficulties. The group dynamic also has a positive effect in encouraging the children to work cooperatively, to learn to take turns and to develop listening and observational skills. The assessment procedure used at Vranch House has been described in Chapter 5. Also detailed there were the criteria a child needs to fulfil in order to attend for regular therapy. After this assessment, he may be offered individual physiotherapy and/or occupational therapy sessions at Vranch House.

Regular weekly therapy groups

At the time of writing there are two types of regular groups. The groups are aimed to give a one-off intensive boost to children aged six to ten years old. There are usually between six and nine in a group with a high staff to child ratio. An additional benefit has been that the parents have used these sessions for informal networking when they drop off and pick up children at the beginning and end of sessions. A report is given on areas to work on and individual goals are set at the end of the period.

FINE AND GROSS MOTOR GROUP

This group is for children aged between six and eight years old and lasts for six weeks. The children attend for a one-and-a-half-hour session every week. There are six, seven or eight pupils per group.

The aims for this group are:

- To evaluate the child's gross and fine motor skills.

- To facilitate the development of the child's fine and gross motor skills.

- To develop the child's self-esteem.

- To enhance listening skills and ability to respond to instructions.

- To develop the child's ability to behave cooperatively in a group.

Other skills include:

- Listening to instructions.

- Following instructions correctly.

- Taking turns.

- Listening while others speak.

- Sitting still.

- Developing a working knowledge of directions such as up/down, behind/in front, forwards/backwards, etc.

- Developing spatial awareness – moving around a stationary environment, moving around a moving environment (with other people).

- Developing body awareness – using different body parts in a controlled way.

- Becoming aware of one's own body and its relationship to the surroundings and other people.

- Working cooperatively in a small group – sharing resources.

- Developing self-evaluation – judging what they have done particularly well.

- Developing self-esteem and self-confidence.

FINE MOTOR GROUP

This group is for children aged between seven and ten years old and lasts for six weeks. The children attend for one hour a week. There are usually six pupils per group. The fine motor groups work on hand function skills. Activities are designed to improve core stability, postural stability, handwriting skills and the skills needed for creative work. There is a particular focus on handwriting skills including monitoring the child's posture and pencil grip.

The session starts with a warm-up activity focusing on gross motor skills including core stability, followed by a multisensory activity related to the theme of the day. Next the pupils complete handwriting activities followed by a creative activity which includes the use of scissors, rulers, cutlery and may involve collage, papier mâché, sandwich making or a similar activity.

The aims for this group are:

- To facilitate the development of the child's fine motor skills.

- To develop the child's core stability.

- To establish good writing posture.

- To develop the child's ability to form letters correctly.

- To develop fluency and accuracy of pencil control.

- To develop the effective use of cutlery.

- To develop the child's self-esteem.

- To help the child to develop listening skills and ability to respond to instructions.

- To develop the child's ability to behave cooperatively in a group situation.

Other skills include:

- Developing attention and concentration.

- Listening to instructions.

- Following instructions correctly.

- Taking turns.

- Listening while others speak.

- Taking pride in presentation.

- Sitting still.

- Working cooperatively in a small group – sharing resources.

- Developing self-evaluation – judging what they have done particularly well.

- Developing self-esteem and self-confidence.

The above aims, activities and skills for both groups are taken from an information leaflet and programme given to parents and carers (Vranch House 2009).

HOME CHALLENGES
At the end of each session children will be given a gross and fine motor task to practise at home each day of the week and bring to the next session.

THE FINAL SESSION
For the final session parents and carers are invited to discuss the child's progress with the therapists. Goals are set and the child's future therapy needs are discussed. This might be an individual follow-up review or a home programme. The parents and carers also attend the final session to see their children demonstrate the activities they have been working on during the programme. This includes ball skills, core stability and table-top activities (e.g. writing, scissor skills, making sandwiches). The children are also presented with their certificates at the end of the programme.

Other support provided by the Vranch House team

- Home and school exercise programmes.

- Advice about special equipment.

- Liaison with, and advice to, schools, usually via the SENCO.

- Liaison with the child's community occupational therapist, regarding specialist equipment at home or in school.

- Liaison with the child's community occupational therapist providing an intervention programme for children with sensory pathway needs.

- Regular contact with parents.

- Coordination of medical and educational services – for example, organizing reports from therapy and school staff for paediatric clinics, or arranging for the therapist to contribute to statements of special educational needs and annual reviews.

Group observations

The last session of two six-week fine motor groups were observed. There were five children in each group, all boys aged between seven and nine years old. The groups were led by a senior occupational therapist supported by two assistants. All the children had a parent or close relative observing the final session. The therapist talked to the children about what they were going to show their parents first and briefly went through some of the activities with them. Then the parents were invited to observe the group.

WARM-UP

The children did a warm-up demonstrating a number of gross motor activities designed to strengthen their shoulders, hips and pelvis and generally improve their core stability.

CRAB FOOTBALL

This activity involved all the children moving on all fours with their chest towards the ceiling (keeping their bottoms up) while passing a football to each other (Photo 2). Taking turns was also part of this activity.

Photo 2

MOVING MATS INTO POSITION

The children were asked to move the mats and position them correctly on the floor in a line next to each other. They were then asked to line up on the mats (lying down) with no more than two on each mat. These tasks were helpful in improving organizational and thinking skills. The therapist suggested to parents that similar activities could be done at home such as taking washing outside and hanging items on the clothes line.

ADAPTED PRESS-UPS

The children were in a four-point kneeling position. Hands and knees were equally apart. They then moved their nose carefully towards the ground while bending their elbows and maintaining a position on all fours (Photos 3 and 4). This is a good activity for strengthening the shoulders and arms.

BALLOON VOLLEYBALL

The children formed two teams and faced each other across the mats. The children were in a high kneeling position and then put one foot forward. In this position they aimed the balloon from one team to another with a raised hand (Photos 5, 6 and 7). The therapist told the parents that this was a good position for children to practise when doing activities such as watching television (i.e. high kneeling). The children are encouraged to keep their bodies in a firm, stable position.

Photo 3

Photo 4

Photo 5

Photo 6

Photo 7

OTHER ACTIVITIES ON THE MATS

First the children knelt on all fours with their arms straight and legs and arms forming right angles to the ground in the same way as they had in the preparation for the adapted press-ups (Photo 8). Next they lay flat on their backs in a symmetrical position (Photo 9), and then bent their knees, with knees pointing upwards (Photo 10). They then lifted their bottoms off the mat to make 'bridges' (Photo 11). From this position, if they were steady enough, they were encouraged to lift a straight leg (Photo 12). Next they put their hands to their sides in an 'aeroplane' position while lying flat on their stomachs and raising their heads. At all times the children were given simple, clear verbal instructions.

Photo 8

Photo 9

Photo 10

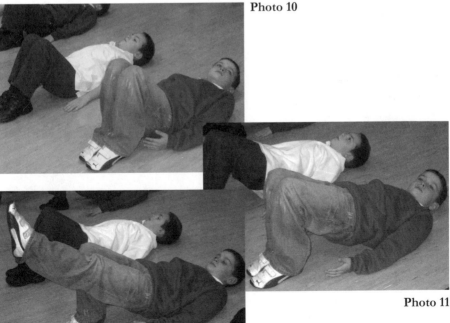

Photo 11

Photo 12

WRITING ACTIVITY

For this activity the children were sitting at tables. During the programme it had been agreed with the individual child whether a sloping board or pencil grip would help them. There were a variety of different types of pencil grips available. Most of the children had decided to use a sloping board or pencil grip. Before starting the therapist ensured that the children were sitting in a good position with their bottom in the middle of the seat and feet flat on the floor. She asked them how they should be sitting and they told her 'Sit in the middle'; some children demonstrated how to achieve this by pushing down with their arms on the chair seat and lifting their bottom to the centre of the chair. They were reminded to keep their feet flat on the floor by being asked to stamp their feet to check they were in the right position. The therapist asked them to check that their sloping boards or worksheets were at the correct angle (not straight in front of them but at about a 45-degree angle). They were reminded to use their helping hand by having a *smiley* face drawn on their paper so that it was in the correct position for them to cover it with their non-writing hand. The children then worked on patterns to improve fluency and flow in writing letters. They were given lines on their paper to guide them (Photos 13, 14 and 15). The therapist reminded them that she was looking for 'quality not quantity'. One child had particular difficulties in crossing midline (i.e. for his left writing hand to move to the right side of the paper). The therapist asked him to close his eyes and supported his hand and took his hand through the pattern so that he could feel it using his kinaesthetic sense. This helped him to then continue the pattern independently.

Photo 13

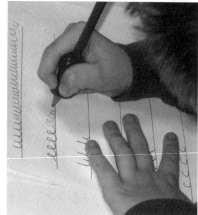

Photo 14

Photo 15

CUTTING SKILLS

The children were given a warning that scissors are sharp and they need to take care. The scissors used were suitable for right- and left-handed children. They were told, 'Thumbs up for scissors'. This put their hands in a good position to pick up the scissors (Photo 16). The pupils used a worksheet to cut out shapes and again were encouraged to use a helping hand (Photo 17).

Photo 16

Photo 17

MAKING LETTERS USING WOODEN STICKS

The children were given wooden sticks and asked to make letters from them, for example A, K (Photos 18 and 19). These letters involve diagonals which are the most perceptually challenging direction to reproduce.

Photo 18

Photo 19

SANDWICH MAKING

The children washed their hands first and took turns to pass the plates and knives around the table to each other. The therapist reminded them of the three rules which were:

- good looking
- good listening
- still hands.

The task involved the following stages:

- Holding the knife correctly by putting the index finger (Peter Pointer) on the back of the blade.
- Spreading the butter towards the body with the knife in one hand and using the other 'helping' hand to hold the plate and bread.
- Putting a slice of cheese on the bread and/or spreading some jam on it (the children were given the choice).
- Putting the pieces of bread together.
- Cutting the sandwich in half across the middle and then again into quarters.

The task had been clearly broken down and each step was demonstrated by an assistant so the children had to watch and copy (Photos 20, 21 and 22). The children were also warned about using knives correctly for health and safety reasons. The sandwiches were then eaten with gusto and if they were not able to eat all of their sandwich, they had the option of taking the rest home in a paper bag.

Photo 20

Photo 21

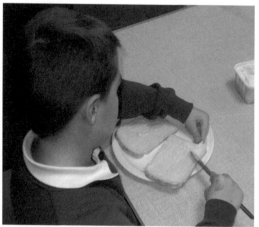

Photo 22

Photo 23

POURING A DRINK

The children were asked which flavour drink they would like (e.g. blackcurrant, orange or water). If they wanted a flavour, the juice was put into their cup. They then individually poured water from a jug into their cups (Photo 23). They were reminded not to overfill their cups. They all managed to do this without spilling any liquid but used a great deal of concentration in order to achieve the activity. Following this they had their drink with their sandwich. Then they were given a paper napkin in order to wipe their hands.

Photo 24

PRESENTATION

At the end of the session each of the children were presented with their folder of work and their certificate (Photo 24). This was done formally with the child shaking hands with the therapist and all the parents and children applauding. Their folders contained their completed writing activity sheets, cutting and ruler skills activities and some special lined paper to help them with their writing in the future. They also took home the model which they had made during the sessions, in this case a pot or pig which they had made from papier mâché and then painted and decorated.

THE BENEFITS OF THERAPY

Children often develop greater confidence when they find they are able to do something they could not do previously. This confidence can often transfer to other settings such as school and home. They also feel less isolated after joining a group and meeting children with similar difficulties.

Sophie, aged seven

Sophie used to be very, very quiet and she's much more outgoing now – she's much more confident. That is definitely since she's been going into Vranch House, she's really come out of her shell. She'd sort of hide behind me, if anyone spoke to her, and now she'll be at the door shouting out 'Hello' to the neighbours.

Emma, aged ten

She's gained a lot of confidence since she's been in Vranch House. The first day she went in, she was awfully nervous about going in when we left her. When we came back she got in the car and said, 'There are bigger boys there than I am and they can't write either.' She just changed once she found out there were other children who could not do things. In school they used to colour and write and used to go ahead of her, all the young ones, and she was getting left behind.

Previously her mother reported that Emma was unwilling to attend her primary school, but now she is quite enthusiastic about going to school and her self-confidence has improved.

Paul, aged eight

Paul refused to go to school during his first term. When he started at Vranch House he was six years old, and 'It used to be the highlight of his week.' He has learned to swim and is very confident in water. His primary school now understand his difficulties, and he has had additional support from a learning support assistant. Now he is working well in school and his maths and reading have both improved.

Lisa, aged nine

Lisa's mother reported that her PE skills have improved and also her swimming ability.[2] 'That's one area where she really outshines Caroline [her younger sister], and it's just so lovely for her to have that one thing she is really good at and that Caroline finds more difficult.' She also said that Lisa's self-esteem has improved and that this has become more apparent as she has become older, even though the demands of school have become greater.

---

2   Since 2005 swimming has no longer been part of the activity programme for groups.

Chapter 10

LEAVING SCHOOL

Higher Education, Careers and Adult Life

Does the dyspraxia continue as a young person matures? Portwood (1998, p.17) says, 'Dyspraxia is not a condition that one simply "grows out of". Dyspraxic children become dyspraxic adults. Intervention can be effective at any age.' Researchers have come up with differing results in long-term studies.

Losse *et al.* (1991) carried out a study of 17 children identified by teachers as having poor motor coordination at 6 years of age and followed up again at 16. 'The results suggest that the majority of children still have difficulties with motor coordination, have poor self-concept and are experiencing problems of various kinds in school' (Losse *et al.* 1991, p.67). However, they reported differences in the ways that individual children learned coping strategies to deal with their difficulties.

Cantell, Smyth and Ahonen (1994) carried out a similar study in Finland, identifying children at 5 years of age and following up 81 of them at 15. They found that over half (54%) did not differ significantly from the control group: they were performing well in school, were ambitious and were taking part in social sports. Although they were still found to have some difficulties with motor tasks, some of the young people in this group were very keen on team sports and had spent a great deal of time taking part in them. The other 46 per cent differed from the control group on both motor and perceptual tasks. This group had fewer social activities, lower academic ambitions and poorer self-esteem.

So it is likely that many dyspraxic children do overcome their early motor difficulties and develop coping strategies to deal effectively with organizational problems, but some do not. None of the children in the

Losse *et al.* (1991) study took part in long-term intervention programmes, and it is not clear whether the Finnish children did so. Nowadays there is far greater awareness of dyspraxia and movement difficulties, so it is to be hoped that many more children will succeed, become more confident and develop good self-esteem. One of the most often expressed comments from Vranch House parents is that, following an intervention programme, their child has become more self-confident both at home and at school.

LEAVING SCHOOL AND BEYOND

The young dyspraxic adult is likely to avoid doing any jobs, hobbies or other activities that involve things that are difficult, such as writing, performing coordination skills and competitive sport. This is not unusual – most adults tend to make use of their strengths and avoid those activities that they know they do less well. The young dyspraxic person should be encouraged to develop strategies that minimize his difficulties. Sound career advice should be taken. Realistic expectations are important but should not restrict the ambitious and determined individual (see case study on p.116).

SOME TIPS FOR SCHOOL-LEAVERS
Writing

Use a computer or laptop. Check out various keyboards and mice. There are many available, and you can usually try them out at local computer stores. You can get keyboards that are larger or smaller than a normal keyboard as well as specially ergonomically designed ones. Use a spell check program. If you do not have speech problems, try out voice-activated word-processing software. Andy (see p.118) found a handwriting recognition program invaluable in taking lecture notes at university.

Use a personal organizer/planner/calendar

Make a note of all appointments, personal as well as business. Use colour-coding for different appointments, for example dental and medical appointments in red, social arrangements in blue, work appointments in green, and so on. It's useful to keep two types of planners or organizers – a small one that you keep with you at all times, and a larger one for your kitchen or bedroom wall. Use highlighters or stickers for the colours.

Allow plenty of time

Make sure you set your alarm to give you plenty of time to get ready in the mornings. Plan your routes to work or business appointments to make sure you have enough time. Get your clothes and the things you need to take for work or college ready the night before.

Use notepads or a tape-recorder

- Keep a notepad by your bed in case things you have forgotten come to you in the middle of the night.

- Make shopping lists. Go round the kitchen and check what you need before you go shopping.

- If you are going on holiday, write down everything you need to take with you.

- If you find it tiring to write or your writing is difficult to read, use a digital voice recorder or the recorder on your mobile phone, if you have one.

Exercise regularly and keep fit

You may never play competitive team games, but there are many other ways of keeping fit which are non-competitive but enjoyable:

- Walking – especially with a dog.

- Rambling – join a ramblers' club.

- Swimming.

- Doing a personal fitness programme at your local gym.

- Cycling.

- Sports such as tai chi, yoga, Taekwon-Do, judo.

- Water sports.

Be positive!

Concentrate on the things you do well. Everyone has different strengths and weaknesses. We cannot all walk tightropes or swing from trapezes, but we can make the best of our talents. We can also contribute to society in a positive way. Do some voluntary work for a charity or help out at the local day centre for elderly people. People who have struggled to overcome difficulties themselves often have a special understanding of those who are disadvantaged in some way and can make excellent coaches.

ANDY: A CASE STUDY

Andy is currently in his second year at university and studying applied IT. Andy's university is a three-hour journey from home so he comes home only for the occasional weekend during term time. IT was not his first choice and because of his interest in canoeing and kayaking he would have preferred to pursue a career in outdoor education. However he realized this was not a viable option financially due to the seasonal nature of the work.

Andy has obtained some extra support through the Disabled Students' Allowance (DSA). He and his father researched how he could get the DSA. Andy was required to have a 'needs assessment' and decided to go back to Vranch House and see the therapist he had seen when he was in Year 7. He said, 'I thought I may as well go back to the same people as they've already got a file on me and all they need to do is update it a bit and send it on to the local authority.'

Through the DSA he received a laptop computer, a book allowance for non-core textbooks, a photocopying allowance and a consumables allowance for stationery and similar items. He also gets ten hours of one-to-one tuition with a tutor based at the university. This ten-hour period works out overall as one hour per week and he has to renew the claim every semester. His allowances are reimbursed on the production of receipts.

He has found the whole procedure of obtaining the allowance, getting his laptop, reimbursement for resources and renewing his tuition very laborious, with delays and forms going backwards and forwards between the university and the local authority. For example, he said:

> I'm not too impressed with how the local authority are managing it because I've now got to go back on Monday to the Admissions Office and get them to sign a bit of paper to say that I've enrolled at the university and that I'm on my course and I'm doing lectures. Then I have to send it back to the local authority so I can get reimbursed for bits and pieces whereas they should be able to just look on the computer for student loans and see that I've already enrolled because I've been paid my student loan.

This event was several weeks into the new semester. When requesting more one-to-one tuition Andy said:

We send off the request for more hours during week 7 or 8 of the semester. Each teaching semester is 12 weeks long and during the first semester I didn't actually get told that I had any more hours until the week I was going home. It doesn't also help that the phone line to the department is only open two hours a day during the week from 11 till 1.

From talking with other people at his university he has found that students from different local authority areas have had varying experiences, with some students receiving their laptops before the beginning of term.

Andy found all the items funded by the DSA extremely helpful at university but says:

It all depends on the recommendations of the Access Centre because not only do you have to have a bit of paper saying that you've got dyspraxia for example in my case, from a recognized institute such as Vranch House, you've then got to go to an Access Centre and show your bit of paper to the assessor. You then say what you want from the DSA. Then they will make recommendations to the county council funding body who will then say 'yea' or 'nay' to what they decide to fund.

I asked Andy if one hour a week was sufficient and he said:

That's more than enough but unfortunately it's right at the beginning of the week before my lectures. My lectures start at 10am on a Tuesday but my tutorial with the tutor is 9am on the Tuesday which is before I get any work given. I find I work better in the mornings. I can concentrate more if I've just rolled out of bed say 10 or 20 minutes or even up to a couple of hours later than I can at 4 or 5 in the afternoon. When you get to that point in the afternoon you just want to go home. Examswise I've been lucky so far they've all been 10 or 11am starts.

Andy agreed that it would be difficult for him if he had exams in the afternoons: 'You just don't want to do them if you can't concentrate.' Andy also gets 20 per cent extra time for his exams if he needs it.

Andy talked about other special equipment he has found helpful at university. Most of the lecturers print out their PowerPoint notes and hand them out and also make them available on the university website. Occasionally he has found it necessary to take lecture notes and he has found a handwriting recognition memory stick on the Internet which has been extremely helpful.

You just stick it up at the top of your page and turn it on and it's got a special pen so that when you're writing it transmits it to a reader. It creates a file on a USB memory stick so you can put it on to any computer and it will try to interpret your handwriting and translate it straight into text.

Using a laptop to directly type notes in lectures has not proved practical because a laptop is heavy to carry around and there are not always power sockets available in the lecture theatres. The handwriting recognition device is much smaller and lighter and less obtrusive. Andy has never found speech recognition software helpful. He does not really like talking into a voice recorder. This would be impractical during lectures and he says that it is easier to 'train' the handwriting recognition programme to recognize your handwriting than 'training' the speech recognition software to recognize your speech.

Andy has found that the university support infrastructure has worked extremely well. He has his weekly one-to-one tuition and in addition the support department is only a short walk across the campus where he can drop in and talk to someone if he has a problem.

During his individual sessions he said, 'We have a talk at the beginning of each semester and then set goals to achieve. I've been working on punctuation and memory tasks as well as bringing in bits of work to just go through with her.' His tutor supports a number of students with a range of difficulties at the university including dyspraxia and dyslexia. During his first year Andy found the tuition especially helpful:

> Because it was my first year I wasn't quite sure about how to do things, especially when it came nearer the end of the year when I was rushing to get all these thousand word reports in. I'd never seen so many words in one place before and I wasn't quite sure how to lay it out and all that, so she helped me do that and helped me to proof read it.

One area Andy is currently working on is memory techniques:

> We had eight picture cards last week and I put them into groups and had to create a story out of them. Then we flipped them over and I had to try to remember them. That was the visual part and then she went one step further and assigned auditory descriptions to each of them. Then we went through the visual and auditory associations for each of the cards. After this she would say, 'Fifth one – what's the auditory association?' and I would have to think what it was.

Andy commented, 'My memory's not brilliant but it's not so bad that I have forgotten to hand in assignments.'

Andy's tutor has also helped him plan his work throughout the year by creating with him a list of all his modules and milestones such as assignment submission dates. He created columns for each of the 12 weeks throughout each semester and then put the milestones in boxes within the columns so that he is able to see at a glance the order of assignments and when they are due in.

Usually Andy does not have a problem with spelling but sometimes he finds he has written the wrong word in a document. He said:

> If people are talking and I'm not really concentrating I can put in stuff that shouldn't be there. For example when I was typing for you to get here instead of putting 'and turn right at the mini roundabout' I put 'turn left at the *razor*' because they were talking about something to do with razors while I was sitting in the lounge typing it up. Then when I got back to it and saw that I'd put *razor* in I changed it.

Andy said, 'My handwriting is almost as bad as a doctor's!' However, he can now write fairly neatly as long as he has a good quality pen and is not rushed.

Summer vacation work

Since Andy left his secondary school he has been back working as a paid employee during two summer vacations with the school site staff. Quite a lot of building work was being done at the school and he worked with the two site staff moving equipment to the new buildings.

Kayaking

Andy has enjoyed kayaking since he was in primary school and has recently achieved his level 1 coaching qualification. He coaches at the university club and at a club near his home. He has been involved in some slalom and sprint races at university but his local club is less competitive and more involved in training young people to enjoy kayaking. Andy said that kayaking has improved his coordination skills:

> You have to have some sort of hand–eye coordination to be able to do some of the skills and I think it has partly helped in the improvement of that and the lessening of the effect of the dyspraxia.

He advises other young people with dyspraxia to take up a sport:

Doing an activity such as that has definitely helped even if it's just playing a bit of five a side once a week, anything's better than nothing. So if you're playing football for example, volunteer to be goalie. You've got balls pelted at you that you've got to try and save. You've got to try and train your brain to judge distances a lot better. Driving has also helped: I've had a full licence for about two and a half years now.

DISABLED STUDENTS' ALLOWANCES

Disabled Students' Allowances are to support students with disabilities or specific learning difficulties in the UK. They are additional to the normal student loans and do not have to be repaid. They are to cover additional expenses so that students with a disability can study on an equal basis. The allowances can be used for special equipment such as a laptop computer, a non-medical helper such as a note-taker or reader, extra travel costs and other resources such as audio tapes. See Appendix 2 for the website address where you can get full information and information on how to apply. There are a range of grants available to disabled students in the US. Full details can be found on the College Scholarships website: www.collegescholarships. org/grants/disabilities.htm.

Appendix 1

USEFUL INFORMATION

UK GOVERNMENT PUBLICATIONS AND WEBSITES

All websites were accessed on 22 February 2010.

Directgov

www.direct.gov.uk

This UK government website gives information on all sorts of aspects of education in a very accessible way.

Every Child Matters

www.dcsf.gov.uk/everychildmatters

This website is devoted to all aspects of *Every Child Matters*.

National Strategies

http://nationalstrategies.standards.dcsf.gov.uk

This website gives information on the UK National Curriculum and the Early Years Foundation Stage.

Special Educational Needs (SEN) – a Guide for Parents and Carers (revised 2009)

This booklet explains the procedure of statutory assessment, statements of special educational needs, annual reviews and Special Educational Needs Tribunals. There is a very helpful list of addresses and telephone numbers at the back of the leaflet, including those of advisory and help centres and special interest groups. Available from: DCSF Publications, PO Box 5050, Sherwood Park, Annersley, Nottingham NG15 0DJ. Tel. 0845 602 2260. Also available from: www.teachernet.gov.uk

US GOVERNMENT PUBLICATIONS AND WEBSITES
Communicating with Your Child's School Through Letter Writing. A Parent's Guide (2nd Edition)

This useful leaflet for parents is available from NICHCY and can be downloaded from the website, www.nichcy.org. The leaflet written by Rebhorn and Kupper (2002) explains to parents how to go through the assessment procedure under the Individuals with Disabilities Education Act.

Head Start

www.acf.hhs.gov/programs/ohs

This is the website of The Office for Head Start which comes under the US Department of Health and Human Services. There is detailed information about the Head Start program and research projects associated with it.

Healthier US School challenge

www.fns.usda.gov/tn/healthierus/index.html

Information about the Healthier US School Challenge and how schools can become a Team Nutrition School.

Let's Move

www.letsmove.org

This is the Let's Move website to help parents and teachers to improve the fitness and well-being for children in the US.

National Dissemination Center for Children with Disabilities

www.nichcy.org

NICHCY stands for the National Dissemination Center for Children with Disabilities. This is the official US site for information on children and young people with disabilities, IDEA (the law authorizing special education) and 'No Child Left Behind' with regard to children with disabilities. There are lots of useful online publications for parents on special education and types of difficulties and the special education system. The site is available in English and Spanish. Address: NICHCY, 1825 Connecticut Ave NW, Suite 700, Washington, DC 20009. Tel: (800) 695-0285, email: nichcy@aed.org.

US Department of Education

www.ed.gov

Official website of US Department of Education with information about government acts, policy and initiatives on education.

SPECIAL EQUIPMENT

Dycem mats are washable non-slip mats for fixing items such as plates or books to the table. They come in various sizes and shapes, and are available in rolls from which lengths can be cut off. Pencil grips are small rubber or plastic grips which fit on to a pencil or pen to provide support. They come in a range of shapes (triangular or rounded) and are designed to promote a good tripod pencil grip. Triangular pencils are also designed to promote a good functional pencil grip. Plastazote tubing (supplied in one-metre lengths) can be cut to size and used to provide a larger grip for pencils, pens, brushes and cutlery. Various scissors are available, including spring-loaded and dual control scissors. All available from: Nottingham Rehab Supplies, Clinitron House, Excelsior Road, Ashby De La Zouch, Leicestershire LE65 1JG. Tel. 0845 120 4522. Website: www.nrs-uk.co.uk

WriteAngle sloping tabletop boards: clear perspex, portable, fixed-height writing slope. Available from: Posturite (UK) Ltd, The Mill, Berwick, East Sussex BN26 6SZ. Tel. 0845 345 0010. Website: www.posturite.co.uk

OT Practice Buyers Guide. Downloadable from the website of the American Occupational Therapy Association (AOTA). Website: www.aota.org/BuyersGuide.aspx

IDEAS FOR PE

Leap into Life!

Devon Curriculum Services (2007) *Leap into Life! A Resource for Delivery of Physical Literacy at Foundation Stage and Key Stage 1* is published by Devon Curriculum Services (DCS). Available from DCS, Great Moor House, PO Box 266, Exeter EX2 7XZ. Tel. 01392 384839. Email: dcs.pubs@devon.gov.uk

Special Needs Activities

Knight, E. (1992) *Special Needs Activities*. Curriculum Services for Physical Education, Hertfordshire County Council. A booklet of flipcards giving ideas for PE in school. Available from: Action Point, Wheathampstead Education Centre, Butterfield Road, Wheathampstead, Herts AL4 8PY. Tel. 01582 830251.

BOOKS FOR ACTION AND MOVEMENT SONGS

Okki-tocki-unga

Harrop, B., Friend, L. and Gadsby, D. (1976) *Okki-tocki-unga*. London: A. & C. Black. Action songs for children with piano accompaniment.

Apuskidu

Harrop, B., Blakely, P. and Gadsby, D. (1975) *Apuskidu*. London: A. & C. Black. Songs for children with piano accompaniment. These are not specifically action or movement songs, but some can be used in this way, e.g. 'If you're happy and you know it', 'Ten in the bed' and 'One potato, two potato'.

This Little Puffin

Matterson, E. (1991) *This Little Puffin*. London: Penguin.
This book contains a large number of action-and-movement songs and rhymes; the songs have simple melody lines written out, not full accompaniment.

ONLINE RESOURCE
Dance Mat Typing

This is a free online program to teach children touch typing skills. It is fun, interactive and has four graded levels. Website: www.bbc.co.uk/schools/typing

Appendix 2

USEFUL ADDRESSES
AND WEBSITES

All websites were accessed on 22 February 2010.

UK ADDRESSES AND WEBSITES
AbilityNet
AbilityNet is a national charity which specializes in helping adults and children with disabilities in using computers and the Internet by adapting and adjusting technology.

Tel. 0800 269545 (if you call from home) or 01926 312847 (if you call from work). Email: enquiries@abilitynet.org.uk. Website: www.abilitynet.org.uk

Advisory Centre for Education (ACE)
ACE is an independent national education advice centre which offers confidential advice to parents. It also publishes a number of guides and handbooks relating to various areas of education.

Advisory Centre for Education, 1b Aberdeen Studios, 22–24 Highbury Grove, London N5 2DQ. General Advice Line: Freephone 0808 800 5793 (Monday to Friday, 10am to 5pm). Website: www.ace-ed.org.uk

AFASIC
AFASIC represents children and young adults with communication impairments. The organization provides support for parents, carers and professionals working with these children through conferences, activity weeks, summer schools, regular newsletters and local support groups.

AFASIC, First Floor, 20 Bowling Green Lane, London EC1R 0BD. Helpline: 0845 355 5577 (Monday to Friday, 10.30am to 2.30pm). Website: www.afasic.org.uk

British Gymnastics

The website gives details of the locations of local clubs.

British Gymnastics, Ford Hall, Littleshall NSC, Newport, Shropshire, TF10 9NB. Tel. 0845 129 7129. Email: information@british-gymnastics.org. Website: www.british-gymnastics.org

Centre for Studies on Inclusive Education (CSIE)

The CSIE gives information and advice about inclusive education. Its activities include working directly with parents, producing publications and free literature about inclusion, organizing conferences and answering queries on the law.

Centre for Studies on Inclusive Education, New Redland Building, Coldharbour Lane, Frenchay, Bristol BS16 1QU. Tel. 0117 328 4007. Email: admin@csie.org.uk. Website: www.csie.org.uk

Children's Legal Centre

This organization gives free advice and information about the laws and policies that affect children.

Children's Legal Centre, University of Essex, Wivenhoe Park, Colchester, Essex CO4 3SQ. Advice Line: 0808 802 0008 (Monday to Friday, 9am to 5pm). Email: clc@essex.ac.uk. Website: www.childrenslegalcentre.com

Contact a Family

Contact a Family aims to encourage mutual support between families whose children have disabilities and special needs by linking them through support groups and newsletters.

Contact a Family, 209–211 City Road, London, EC1V 1JN. Tel. 020 7608 8700. Helpline: 0808 808 3555. Textphone: 0808 808 3556 (Freephone for parents and families: Monday to Friday, 10am to 4pm; Monday also 5.30 to 7.30pm). Email: info@cafamily.org.uk. Website: www.cafamily.org.uk

Council for Disabled Children

Their mission is 'to advance the well-being of all children and young people across every aspect of their lives'.

Council for Disabled Children, 8 Wakley Street, London, EX1V 7QE. General enquiries: Tel. 020 783 6000. Email: enquiries@ncb.org.uk

DASH (Do Activity Stay Healthy)

DASH was developed in Somerset, UK to help increase families' physical activity levels and promote healthy eating. For more information please follow the link below.

Website: www.healthyweight4children.org.uk/resource/item.aspx?RID=59636

Disabled Students' Allowance

To find out about Disabled Students' Allowance and how to apply go to the website below. Then go to Education and Learning and click on the third item – Disabled Students' Allowances (DSAs). From here you can also download a guide to the DSAs application process.

Website: www.Direct.gov.uk/Disability

Dyscovery Centre

The centre offers assessment, treatment and teaching for children, adolescents and adults with dyspraxia and dyslexia.

The Dyscovery Centre, Allt-Yr-Yn Campus, 12 Cathedral Road, Newport, NP20 5DA. Tel. 01633 432330. Email: dyscoverycentre@newport.ac.uk. Website: http://dyscovery.newport.ac.uk/dyscovery/index.aspx

Dyspraxia Foundation

The Dyspraxia Foundation aims to promote the awareness and understanding of dyspraxia and to support individuals and families affected by it. The organization has local groups across the UK and publishes a regular newsletter.

The Dyspraxia Foundation, 8 West Alley, Hitchin, Herts SG5 1EG. Tel. 01462 455016 (administration). Helpline: 01462 454986 (Monday to Friday, 10am to 12 noon). Email: dyspraxia@dyspraxiafoundation.org.uk. Website: www.dyspraxiafoundation.org.uk

Family Fun Fit

Family Fun Fit was developed in Somerset, UK. The main aim of the Family Fun Fit programme is to encourage the school and the family to work together through physical activity and health education to improve children's health.

Website: www.cornwallhealthyschools.org/family-fun-fit

Halliwick Association of Swimming Therapy

This organization arranges courses to train instructors in the methodology and has details of where Halliwick swimming is taught in an area.

The Halliwick Association of Swimming Therapy, c/o The ADKC Centre, Whitstable House, Silchester Road, London W10 6SB. Website: www.halliwick.org.uk

Independent Panel for Special Education Advice (IPSEA)

IPSEA gives independent advice on LAs' legal duties towards children with special educational needs, free professional opinions for parents who disagree with an LA's assessment of their child's special educational needs, and free representation at the Special Educational Needs Tribunal.

IPSEA, 6 Carlow Mews, Woodbridge, Suffolk IP12 1EA. Tel. 01394 446575. General Advice Line: 0800 018 4016 (Monday to Friday, 10am to 4pm, plus Monday to Thursday, 7pm to 9pm). Tribunal Helpline: 0845 602 9579 (Monday to Thursday 10am to 1pm). Website: www.ipsea.org.uk

National Association of Special Educational Needs

The aims of NASEN are to promote the interests of those with exceptional learning needs and/or disabilities; to provide a forum for those actively involved with exceptional learning needs and/or disabilities; and to contribute to the formulation and development of policy. NASEN publishes two journals and a magazine/newsletter.

NASEN House, 4–5 Amber Business Village, Amber Close, Amington, Tamworth B77 4RP. Tel. 01827 311500. Email: welcome@nasen.org.uk. Website: www.nasen.org.uk

National Parent Partnership Network

Parent Partnership Services give support to parents and carers of children and young people with special educational needs. In particular they will support parents going through the statutory assessment (statementing) procedure. They provide confidential and impartial advice.

National Parent Partnership Network, 8 Wakley Street, London EC1V 7QE. Tel. 020 7843 6058. Email: nppn@ncb.org.uk. Website: www.parent-partnership.org.uk

National Portage Association

Portage is a home-visiting service for pre-school children with special needs. Portage home visitors assess children's needs and work together with parents on a home-based teaching programme. Local contact telephone numbers can be found on the website.

National Portage Association, Kings Court, 17 School Road, Hall Green, Birmingham B28 8JG. Website: www.portage.org.uk

Network 81

Network 81 is a national organization of parents of children with special educational needs and gives advice on various issues relating to education such as statementing and the *Code of Practice*.

Network 81, 1–7 Woodfield Terrace, Chapel Hill, Stansted, Essex CM24 8AJ. Helpline: 0845 077 4055. Email: info@network81.org. Website: www.network81.org

Parents for Inclusion

Parents for Inclusion is an association of parents of children with disabilities who believe in all children's entitlement to a good education in their local mainstream school. The helpline is run by trained parents to advise other parents on issues relating to inclusion.

Parents for Inclusion, 336 Brixton Road, London, London SW9 7AA. Tel. 020 7735 7735. Helpline: 0800 652 3145. Website: www.parentsforinclusion.org

Taekwon-Do

Information about Taekwon-Do instruction can be obtained from the UK Taekwon-Do Association.

Website: www.ukta.com

Tumble Tots, Gymbabes and Gymbobs
The website gives contact information for local groups.

Tumble Tots (UK) Limited, Blue Bird Park, Bromsgrove Road, Hunnington, Halesowen, West Midlands B62 OTT. Tel. 0121 585 7003. Website: www. tumbletots.com

Youth Sport Trust
The Youth Sport Trust supports a number of initiatives such as the TOP programmes for a range of age groups: Active Play for 4 – 7 year olds; Start to Play for 0–5 year olds.

Youth Sport Trust, Sport Park, 3 Oakwood Drive, Loughborough, Leicestershire LE11 3QF. Tel. 01509 226600. Email: info@youthsporttrust.org. Website: www.youthsporttrust.org

US WEBSITES
Campaign for Better Nutrition
Campaign for better nutrition for children at school and at home.

Website: http://campaignforbetternutrition.org/home.html

Circle of Friends
More information about how Circle of Friends started and the social skills program for inclusion.

Website: www.circleofriends.org

Dyspraxia USA
Website of Dyspraxia USA for those with dyspraxia and their families.

Website: www.dyspraxiausa.org

Grants and Scholarships for Students with Disabilities
This website gives information on the range of grants and scholarships available for students with disabilities.

Website: www.collegescholarships.org/grants/disabilities.htm

My Gym

Find out where the nearest My Gym club is. Different programs are offered for children from 6 weeks to 13 years of age.

Website: www.my-gym.com

Healthy Schools

National environmental health organisation leading National Healthy Schools Day and providing a network for 'healthy' schools.

Website: www.healthyschools.org/who_we_are.html

International Portage Association (IPA)

This website gives background information on the International Portage Association. It is for professionals, parents and individuals interested in the work of Portage.

Email contact: davidshearer@portageinternational.org. Website: http://internationalportageassociation.com

National Association for Sport and Education

The website is a useful resource for teachers and parents including lots of good ideas. The Teachers' Toolbox has many suggestions about physical activities.

Website: www.aahperd.org/naspe

USA Gymnastics

You can locate local gymnastics clubs using this website.

Website: www.usa-gymnastics.org

REFERENCES

American Psychiatric Association (2000) *Diagnostic and Statistical Manual of Mental Disorders DSM-IV-TR* (4th edn). Washington, DC: American Psychiatric Association.

Ayres, A.J. (1972) *Sensory Integration and Learning Disorders*. Los Angeles, CA: Western Psychological Services.

Bailey, G., Sanderson, H., Sweeney, C. and Heaney, B. (2009) *Person Centred Reviews in Adult Services*. Valuing People Support Team, Department of Health. Available at http://valuingpeople.gov.uk/index.jsp, accessed on 22 February 2010.

Barnett, R., Hall, J.D., Kirkby, G.B., Makin, R., Price, D.M. and Williams, D.H. (1989) *Physical Education for Children with Special Educational Needs in Mainstream Education*. Leeds: British Association of Advisers and Lecturers in Physical Education.

Beery, K.E. and Buktenica, N.A. (2004) *Beery-Buktenica Developmental Test of Visual-Motor Integration, Fifth Edition (Beery VM)*. Minneapolis, MN: NCS Pearson Inc.

Boon, M. (1993) *The Integration of Statemented Special Needs Pupils in Ordinary Schools in Lancashire*. MSc thesis, University of Lancaster.

Cantell, M.H., Smyth, M. and Ahonen, T.P. (1994) 'Clumsiness in adolescence: educational, motor, and social outcomes of motor delay detected at 5 years.' *Adapted Physical Activity Quarterly 11*, 2, 115–129.

Connery, V.M., *et al.* (1992) *The Nuffield Centre Dyspraxia Programme*. London: Nuffield Hearing and Speech Centre.

Delaney, B.J., Donnelly, P., News, J. and Haughey, T.J. (2008) *Improving Physical Literacy*. Sport Northern Ireland. Available at www.sportni.net, accessed on 22 February 2010.

Department for Education and Skills (DfES) (2001a) *Special Educational Needs Code of Practice*. Nottingham: DfES (Crown Copyright).

Department for Education and Skills (DfES) (2001b) *Special Educational Needs (SEN) – a Guide for Parents and Carers*. Nottingham: DfES (Crown Copyright).

Department for Education and Skills (DfES) (2003) *The Education (National Curriculum) (Foundation Stage Profile Assessment Arrangements) (England) Order No. 1327 2003*. London: HMSO (Crown Copyright).

Department for Education and Skills (DfES) (2004) *Every Child Matters: Change for Children in Schools*. Nottingham: DfES (Crown Copyright).

Department for Education and Skills (DfES) (2007) *Statutory Framework for the Early Years Foundation Stage*. Nottingham: DfES (Crown Copyright).

Dixon, N.F. (1972) 'The Beginnings of Perception.' In B.M. Foss (ed.) *New Horizons in Psychology 1*. Harmondsworth: Penguin.

Doran, G.T. (1981) 'There's a S.M.A.R.T. way to write management's goals and objectives.' *Management Review 70*, 11, 35–36.

Dorland, W.A.N. (1947) *The American Illustrated Medical Dictionary* (21st edn). Philadelphia, PA: W.B. Saunders.

Dussart, G. (1994) 'Identifying the clumsy child in school: An exploratory study.' *British Journal of Special Education 21*, 2, 81–86.

Dyspraxia Foundation (1996–2009) *What is Dyspraxia?* Hitchin: Dyspraxia Foundation. Available at www.dyspraxiafoundation.org.uk, accessed on 22 February 2010.

Finlayson, A. and Rickard, D. (2001) 'Development of services for children with co-ordination difficulties in Maidstone mainstream schools.' *APCP Journal* December, 9–15.

Gardner, M.F. (1982) *TVPS: Test of Visual-Perceptual Skills (Non-motor)*. San Francisco, CA: Psychological and Educational Publications.

Gardner, M.F. (1996) *Test of Auditory-Perceptual Skills Revised (TAPS-R)*. Hydesville, CA: Psychological and Educational Publications.

Gibson, E.J. and Walk, R.D. (1960) 'The visual cliff.' *Scientific American 202*, 4, 64–71.

Goodenough, F.L. (1926) *Measurement of Intelligence by Drawings*. Chicago, IL: Harcourt, Brace & World.

Gordon, N. and McKinlay, I. (1980) *Helping Clumsy Children*. Edinburgh: Churchill Livingstone.

Harriman, P.L. (1947) *The New Dictionary of Psychology*. New York: Philosophical Library.

Harris, D.B. (1963) *Children's Drawings as Measures of Intellectual Maturity (A Revision and Extension of the Goodenough Draw-a-man Test)*. New York: Harcourt, Brace & World.

Henderson, S.E. and Sugden, D.A. (1992) *The Movement Assessment Battery for Children*. Sidcup: Psychological Corporation, Harcourt Brace Jovanovich.

Henderson, S.E. and Sugden, D.A. (2007) *The Movement Assessment Battery for Children Second Edition (Movement ABC-2)*. Oxford: Psychological Corporation, Pearson. Available at www.psychcorp.co.uk, accessed on 22 February 2010.

Higgs, C., Balyi, I., Way, R., Cardinal, C., Norris, S. and Bluechardt, M. (2008) *Developing Physical Literacy: A Guide for Parents of Children Ages 0 to 12*. Vancouver, BC: Canadian Sport Centre.

Knight, E. (1992) *Special Needs Activities*. Wheathampstead: Curriculum Services for Physical Education, Hertfordshire County Council.

Losse, A., Henderson, S.E., Elliman, D., Hall, D., Knight, E. and Jongmans, M. (1991) 'Clumsiness in children – do they grow out of it? A 10-year follow-up study.' *Developmental Medicine and Child Neurology 33*, 55–68.

McKinlay, I. (1998) 'Foreword: What Is "Dyspraxia"?' In R. Hunt (ed.) *Praxis Makes Perfect II*. Hitchin: Dyspraxia Foundation.

Nash-Wortham, M. and Hunt, J.C. (1997) *Take Time*. Stourbridge: Robinswood Press.

National Institute for Health and Clinical Excellence (NICE) (2009) *Promoting Physical Activity, Active Play and Sport for Pre-school and School-age Children and Young People in Family, Pre-school, School and Community Settings*. NICE Public Health Guidance 17. London: NICE.

O'Beirne, C., Larkin, D. and Cable, T. (1994) 'Coordination problems and anaerobic performance in children.' *Adapted Physical Activity Quarterly 11*, 2, 141–149.

Palmer, S. (2006) *Toxic Childhood*. London: Orion.

PISA (Programme for International Student Assessment) (2003) *Literacy Skills for the World of Tomorrow: Further Results from 2000*. Paris, France: Organization for Economic Cooperation and Development and Unesco Institute for Statistics.

Portwood, M. (1996) *Developmental Dyspraxia: A Manual for Parents and Professionals*. Durham: Durham County Council.

Portwood, M. (1998) 'Developmental Dyspraxia: Identification, Assessment and Intervention.' In R. Hunt (ed.) *Praxis Makes Perfect II*. Hitchin: Dyspraxia Foundation.

Portwood, M. (1999) *Developmental Dyspraxia: Identification and Intervention. A Manual for Parents and Professionals*. London: David Fulton.

Reborn, T. and Kupper, L. (2002) *Communicating with Your Child's School Through Letter Writing. A Parent's Guide (2nd Edition)*. Washington, DC: National Dissemination Center for Children with Disabilities (NICHCY).

Ripley, K. (2001) *Inclusion for Children with Dyspraxia/DCD: A Handbook for Teachers*. London: David Fulton.

Ripley, K., Daines, B. and Barrett, J. (1997) *Dyspraxia: A Guide for Teachers and Parents*. London: David Fulton.

Rosenthal, J. and McCabe, T. (1999) *Dyspraxia Information Sheet. Disorders 8*, 16–26. University of Sydney.

Roussounis, S.H., Gaussen, T.H. and Stratton, P. (1987) 'A 2-year follow-up study of children with motor coordination problems identified at school entry age.' *Child: Care, Health and Development 13*, 6, 377–391.

Sassoon, R. (1998) 'Dealing with Handwriting Problems.' In R. Hunt (ed.) *Praxis Makes Perfect II*. Hitchin: Dyspraxia Foundation.

Shapiro, B. (1991) 'To Understand Dyspraxia.' In *Praxis Makes Perfect*. Hitchin: Dyspraxia Foundation.

Stott, D.H., Moyes, F.A. and Henderson, S.E. (1984) *Test of Motor Impairment: Henderson Revision*. San Antonio, TX: Psychological Corporation.

Sugden, D.A. (2006) *Developmental Coordination Disorder as a Specific Learning Difficulty: Leeds Consensus Statement 2006*. Leeds: Economic and Social Research Council.

Sugden, D.A. (2008) *Developmental Coordination Disorder: DCD Conference, Oslo (2008)*. Leeds: University of Leeds.

Sylvester, S. (1999) *Dyspraxia Evaluation 1999*. Barnstaple: North Devon Health Trust.

Vranch House (2009) *Mainstream School Services, Outreach Therapy Services, Information Leaflet and* Subject Index 61, 87*Programme for Parents and Carers*. Exeter: Therapy Department, Vranch House.

Walker, M. (1976) *The Makaton Vocabulary*. Camberley: Makaton Vocabulary Project.

Wechsler, D. (1990) *Wechsler Pre-school and Primary Scale of Intelligence – Revised UK Edition (WPPSI-RUK)*. London: Psychological Corporation.

Wechsler, D. (1992) *Wechsler Intelligence Scale for Children – Third UK Edition (WISC-IIIUK)*. London: Psychological Corporation.

Wedell, K. (1973) *Learning and Perceptuo-motor Disabilities in Children*. London: John Wiley.

Whitehead, M. (2001) 'The concept of physical literacy.' *European Journal of Physical Education 6*, 2, 127–138.

Williams, C.A., Smith, J. and Ainsley, J. (1999) 'The effects of a physiotherapy intervention programme on children with developmental coorination disorder.' *Association of Paediatric Chartered Physiotherapists Journal 91*, 32–40.

World Health Organization (2007) *International Statistical Classification of Diseases and Related Health Problems (10th Revision)*. Geneva: World Health Organization.

SUBJECT INDEX

AUTHOR INDEX